D0138635

Digital Forensics
Explained

Digital Forensics Explained

Greg Gogolin, Ph.D.

CRC Press
Taylor & Francis Group
Boca Raton   London   New York

CRC Press is an imprint of the
Taylor & Francis Group, an **informa** business

AN AUERBACH BOOK

CRC Press
Taylor & Francis Group
6000 Broken Sound Parkway NW, Suite 300
Boca Raton, FL 33487-2742

© 2013 by Taylor & Francis Group, LLC
CRC Press is an imprint of Taylor & Francis Group, an Informa business

No claim to original U.S. Government works

Version Date: 20121019

International Standard Book Number: 978-1-4398-7495-0 (Hardback)

Library of Congress Cataloging-in-Publication Data

Gogolin, Greg.
    Digital forensics explained / Greg Gogolin.
        p. cm.
    Includes bibliographical references and index.
    ISBN 978-1-4398-7495-0 (hbk. : alk. paper)
    1. Computer crimes--Investigation. 2. Computer security. 3. Computer engineering. I. Title.

HV8079.C65G64 2013
363.250285--dc23   2012032424

Visit the Taylor & Francis Web site at
http://www.taylorandfrancis.com

and the CRC Press Web site at
http://www.crcpress.com

Contents

Preface

Purpose and Approach

Most technical books tend to be tool-centric and often take on a cookbook approach to describing how to use a specific tool. These books often show a series of screen shots illustrating wizards or mouse-click sequences to perform a task. These types of books have their place, but that is not the type of book that I wanted to write. I was after something that explained the concepts of digital forensics and how the pieces fit together—kind of a "do not give someone a fish, but rather teach them how to fish" approach. I was looking to write a book that was not dependent on a version of software or a piece of technology. The challenge in digital forensics is to open your eyes, see the big picture, and think things through before you act. There is more than one way to approach most problems, and as long as you understand the big picture, you are free to use the ways that make the most sense for you.

This book is organized as follows: Chapter 1 starts with an overview of digital forensics and what you should know about it. This chapter goes over the forensic process, what it takes to be an investigator, trends in digital forensics, and some useful resources. Chapter 2 describes approaches and best practices in digital forensics. Much of this is based on what I have learned over the years while conducting investigations as well as on feedback from other investigators. Included are acquisition forms and a sequential process outline to help guide an investigation, as well as a checklist of supplies when responding to an incident. There is often more than one way to perform an investigation, but if you are not sure where to begin, then this chapter should be helpful. Chapter 3 covers the tools that are often used in an examination. This includes commercial tools, free and open-source tools, computer and mobile tools, and things as simple as extension cords.

Internet and e-mail investigations are covered in Chapter 4 and mobile forensics is covered in Chapter 5. Mobile forensics includes cell phones, iPads, music players, and other small devices that are mobile. In many ways, mobile forensics is easier to grasp than computer forensics because there are fewer parts and moving pieces. However, with the rapid advances in smart phone technology, the environment quickly becomes complex. Chapter 6 is the first chapter with a guest author, Gerald Emerick. He covers cloud computing from an architectureal perspective and its impacts on digital forensics. Chapter 7 is written by Detective Jason Otting, and he walks us through a criminal case from start to finish in a very engaging fashion. You can see the case, emotions, and impact layout in front of you in an extremely personal approach.

Cases need to be documented and presented, and they are covered in Chapter 8. A sample summary report from a simple computer investigation is presented, followed by a cover sheet for a cell phone investigation and then a look at an iPad report. The latter part of the chapter covers presentation considerations, and since reporting and presenting are often the end of a case, the chapter concludes with an overview of archiving a case.

Chapters 9 and 10 are the areas that most digital forensics books bypass. Dr. Barbara Ciaramitaro explains why these two chapters are very useful in providing information to help round out an investigation. Earlier in the book I mention that "Facebook" is a keyword search that should be done routinely in most investigations; Chapters 9 and 10 help explain why.

One thing that investigators often face is a suspect who plans ways to make his/her digital activities hard to trace. Velislav Pavlov writes about anti-forensic techniques and technologies in Chapter 11. He is one of those guys that you go to for ideas regarding breaches in security or when you want to learn about something new. Chapter 12 is the study of relationships and putting the pieces of the puzzle together. It is a topic that is not commonly found in digital forensic books or curriculum, but one that I think is central to improving its effectiveness.

Although it is the last chapter in this book, Chapter 13 is the first one that I wrote. Few articles and books speak to the psychological effects related to digital forensics investigations—and I mean primarily the effects on the investigator. If you think about a movie in which something surprising literally made you jump out of your seat, then you have a good idea of the shocking world awaiting an examiner. There are many sleepless nights ahead in digital forensics—thinking about the victims, their families, and yes, the bad guys. Additionally, I wanted to stress ethics because I have seen a lot of unethical things in the digital forensics field—including the behavior of examiners inside and outside of law enforcement. Once you cross the line into the gray area, it is extremely difficult to get back. The last piece in the chapter deals with cultural implications. I find it absolutely confounding how little culture, languages, and a broader view of the world make up the education and training of forensic examiners. Investigators need to learn foreign languages and appreciation of other cultures if they are going to meet the demands of digital forensics.

Preface is the part of the book that I looked forward to writing because although it is the first part of the book, it is that last part to write—which means that a big chunk of work is finished. Writing a book is like training to run a marathon. There is a lot to do before the event, and training does not go exactly as planned. There are injuries and setbacks, days you do not feel like running, and some things that just fall out of your control. Just like training, it always seems there is more you can do—more topics to add, a better way to do something, or some new development that is supposed to transform everything. Bottom line is you cannot do everything—inadvertent errors will be made, you forget to acknowledge someone, or some graphic could have been clearer—but it is time to get to the starting line and run the race. So with that, I hope you find value in *Digital Forensics Explained*. Feedback is always welcome, and with a name like mine, it is pretty easy to find me with Google. Thank you, and best of luck in your future endeavors!

Greg Gogolin

Acknowledgments

Writing a book is no easy task, and no work is truly the result of a single mind. Whether it is developing writing skills, researching material, learning about what to write in a class, or simply having a discussion over a Guinness, a lot of people influence the final product whether everyone realizes it or not.

Writing is always something that has appealed to me, and I received good feedback from coworkers when I'd write up "bread crumb" documents detailing how to use technology, techniques, or business practices prior to my teaching days. That planted the seed that someday I should write a technical book. Rich O'Hanley from Auerbach/Taylor & Francis contacted me after one of my articles ran in *Information Security Journal: A Global Perspective* to see if I was interested in writing a book. Without his initiative—and very high degree of patience—this book would not have happened. It goes without saying that I am very appreciative of Rich and the staff at Taylor & Francis.

Digital forensics is a field that is exploding in detail and need. I am fortunate to work with some talented teachers, technicians, and writers at Ferris State University. I have written some chapters for books edited by Dr. Barbara Ciaramitaro, and she showed me the value in collaborating. She contributed two chapters to this book— "Social Media Forensics" and "Social Engineering Forensics"—and helped keep my spirits up during the dry spells that are a common when writing.

Gerald Emerick and I used to work together in industry, and he was one of the most skilled software architects with whom I had the pleasure of working. When he became a professor at Ferris State University in the fall of 2011—and I was in the midst of one of those dry spells—we discussed the idea of cloud forensics. Rather than a focus on a cookbook approach of applying the forensic tools to cloud situations, stepping back and understanding the cloud technology put the horse back in front of the cart. This book helps a reader understand the big picture of digital forensics;

Jerry's chapter helps you understand the cloud; and taken together, one should be able to apply digital forensic techniques to the cloud.

Velislav Pavlov works in information technology at Ferris State University, and I have had the pleasure of having him in my classroom. The first time he submitted an assignment I thought he had lifted it from NASA or someplace because it was so well done. He is at an unusual level relative to most people when it comes to technical skill. Given his deep knowledge and appreciation for information security and the hacking community, I asked if he would write a chapter on anti-forensics, which I am sure readers will find to be a special treat.

Detective Jason Otting is one of many law enforcement officers I have had in my classroom. It is interesting to have them share their experiences and to help provide insight into the challenges that are part of law enforcement in general and digital aspects of crime in particular. Otting agreed to write a chapter that would walk the reader through a case from start to finish in terms of both procedure and the challenging nature of many digital crimes. Otting is a tremendous resource in the law enforcement community, and I am pleased to count him as a friend.

Thanks to the very talented Detective Rebecca MacArthur of the Michigan State Police for your ideas, sharing your seizure forms for inclusion in this book, and friendship. Your efforts in law enforcement are appreciated by more people than you realize.

Dr. Douglas Blakemore and the students at Ferris State University have provided me with many ideas for the book. Understanding the concepts that are difficult for them to grasp gave me ideas for what needed to be covered. Molly Mostek even went as far as to develop a bibliography for me to leverage and David Schippers, Wendy Hadersbeck, and Erin Gogolin helped to proofread. Thanks to everyone at Ferris. Go Bulldogs!

I have also taught cyber security courses and developed curriculum for the University of Maryland University College (UMUC). This has helped round out my understanding of issues within the federal government and the Department of Defense. Thank you to Alan Carswell, Clay Wilson, Patrick Fitzgibbons, Ping Wang, and the fine students at UMUC.

I have been working on a digital forensic research grant from the National Science Foundation. The project involves recoverability of information from damaged media. I do have a short discussion of this, so I would like to acknowledge the National Science Foundation. This material is based upon work supported by the National Science Foundation under Grant No. 1116268. Any opinions, findings, and conclusions or recommendations expressed in this material are those of the author(s) and do not necessarily reflect the views of the National Science Foundation.

Also, a shout-out to Jesse, Dave, and Shane at Guidance Software. I enjoyed your courses over the years, and they helped shape my digital forensics approach.

As any author knows, the people who make the most significant contributions to any book are the author's family. The contribution may be more a matter of tolerance than anything written, but tolerance for allowing me to spend so much time at the keyboard is an incredible sacrifice. Thank you Lauri, Erin, Isaac, and Seth, and Evan, my angel in the sky, I think of you constantly. Yes, Ike, I can play you a game of one-on-one now. Yes, Erin, I would love to go ride horses. Yes, Seth, I will go swimming. And yes, Lauri—I would love to go out to dinner—just us two! And, yes, everyone, I will leave the computer at home on the next vacation!!

Greg Gogolin

Authors

Dr. Greg Gogolin is a father, as well as a professor at Ferris State University in Big Rapids, Michigan. Greg spent almost twenty years in information technology before becoming a professor at Ferris State University in 1999. He was the primary author of the Bachelor of Science in Information Security & Intelligence and Master of Science in Information Security & Intelligence degrees. Prior to Ferris, he worked as a programmer, database administrator, systems analyst, and project manager at small and multinational corporations. Dr. Gogolin actively consults in information technology and is a licensed private investigator specializing in digital forensics cases. He has degrees in arts, computer information systems, applied biology, computer information systems management, and administration and holds a doctorate from Michigan State University. He has current CISSP, EnCE, and PMP certifications, and is particularly thankful to have the opportunity to teach some of the brightest students in the world in the bachelor of science in information security and intelligence and the master of science in information systems management programs at Ferris State University in Michigan, and the master of science in cyber security at the University of Maryland University Center.

Dr. Gogolin has published in *Information Security Journal*: "A Global Perspective, Digital Investigations, Digital Forensic Practice," and has made chapter contributions to IGI Global's *Mobile Technology Consumption: Opportunities and Challenges; Virtual Worlds and E-Commerce: Technologies and Applications for Building Customer Relationships;* and Nova Science Publisher's *Crime Rates, Types,* and *Hot Spots,* as well as other periodicals. He has presented at many conferences and collaborates on information security and digital forensic issues worldwide. His current research interest is a National Science Foundation–funded inquiry into the recovery of data from damaged media. He is also actively building relationships with other universities worldwide, including Saxion University of Applied Science, the Netherlands.

Dr. Barbara L. Ciaramitaro is an assistant professor with the College of Business at Ferris State University in Big Rapids, Michigan, where she teaches graduate and undergraduate courses on a variety of topics including information security, business intelligence, social media and virtual worlds, and project management. Dr. Ciaramitaro entered the academic world after 30 years of experience in business, including 10 years as an executive with General Motors.

Dr. Ciaramitaro holds a PhD from Nova Southeastern University in information systems with a graduate certificate in information security, an MS from Central Michigan University in software engineering administration, and a BA in psychology from Wayne State University. She is currently working on earning her MBA degree from Ferris State University. Dr. Ciaramitaro has earned several professional certifications including the CISSP (Certified Information System Security Professional), CSSLP (Certified Software System Lifecycle Professional), and PMP (Project Management Professional).

Dr. Ciaramitaro is a frequent speaker and author on topics including information security, social engineering, project management, social media, virtual worlds, and privacy. She edited the book and authored chapters in *Virtual Worlds and E-Commerce: Technologies and Applications for Building Customer Relationships* published by IGI Global in August 2010 and did the same for *Mobile Technology Consumption: Opportunity and Challenges* published by IGI Global in October 2011. She is currently working on her next edited collection for IGI Global focused on cloud security. She is an active member of several professional organizations including ISACA, ISC², IEEE, and the Project Management Institute.

Prof. Gerald Emerick joined the Ferris ISI program as a full-time faculty member in the fall of 2011 after 20 years in the information systems business environment and 10 years as an adjunct faculty member. During his 20 years in information systems, he held many different positions in both large international organizations and small organizations. He has held positions such as management consultant, project manager, software design and development, and database administrator. He actively consults in Internet software design and development as well as in database design and administration.

Professor Emerick earned a master of science degree in computer information systems from Grand Valley State University and a bachelor of business administration degree from Eastern Michigan University in business computer systems. His many professional certifications include Project Management Professional (PMP) and Certified Information Systems Security Professional (CISSP).

Det. Jason Otting is a United States Marine Corps veteran who served from 1994 to 1998 with the 2nd Battalion, 6th Marine Regiment. He ended his military career with the goal of pursuing opportunities in law enforcement. In 2004, he became a deputy with a northern Michigan sheriff's department and in that time worked as an undercover narcotics officer and in the road patrol. In recent years, Otting desired to continue his education at Ferris State University with a specific interest in cyber crime. Seeing an opportunity in the digital forensic field, he completed his bachelor's degree in information security and digital forensics and more recently a master of science in information systems management. Wanting to work in cyber crime investigation, he has recently begun working as a detective in computer crimes.

Prof. Velislav Pavlov is a technology services coordinator for Ferris State University in Grand Rapids, Michigan. Velislav has 10 years of practical experience in information systems and security. He teaches a graduate-level penetration testing course for Ferris State University in Big Rapids, Michigan, and cyber attacks and defenses courses for Excelsior College in Albany, New York. In addition, Velislav has served as a security course developer, subject matter expert, and course reviewer. He holds a bachelor of science in information and computer security from Davenport University, a master of science in information system management from Ferris State University, and CompTIA A+, Security+, and ITILv3 certifications. He has an active membership with ISSA, NAISG, and InfraGuard professional information security organizations. Velislav is also a chapter coauthor on mobile security in *Mobile Technology Consumption: Opportunities and Challenges* premier reference book published by IGI Global in 2012. Some of his current research interests include penetration testing, digital forensics, network intrusion detection, IT compliance and governance, mobile security, and information security awareness.

Contributors

Dr. Barbara L. Ciaramitaro, CISSP, CSSLP, PMP
Information Security & Intelligence
Ferris State University
Big Rapids, Michigan

Prof. Gerald Emerick, PMP, CISSP
Information Security & Intelligence
Ferris State University
Big Rapids, Michigan

Det. Jason Otting, ACE
Computer Crimes Unit
Grand Traverse County Sheriff's
    Department
Traverse City, Michigan

Prof. Velislav Pavlov
Information Technology
Ferris State University
Big Rapids, Michigan

WHAT IS DIGITAL FORENSICS, AND WHAT SHOULD YOU KNOW ABOUT IT?

Introduction

Over the years I have read many technical books that provide screenshots of particular tools and their operations. Whenever a tool is updated, such books become obsolete. This book focuses on the methodologies, techniques, resources, and mind-set that is necessary in understanding the digital forensics process. My philosophy, and that of my chapter contributors, is that an understanding of the process is primary. Adapting that understanding to tools and technologies can then be effectively realized. Attempting to develop high levels of skill with a particular tool or technology before an understanding of the big picture is attained is short-sighted and invites error. Discipline is necessary in any science and digital forensics is no different.

Digital forensics is the application of scientific principles to the process of discovering information from a digital device. A form of digital forensics has been around nearly as early as computers were invented, but forensic capabilities have witnessed many advances in the past years as digital forensic processes have matured and needs have become more prevalent. Digital forensics can involve nearly any digital device, not just computers, although technology often evolves faster than forensic capabilities do. Some of the common areas in which digital forensics is used include computers, printers, cell phones, mobile devices, global positioning systems (GPSs), and storage media. Less common areas include automobile systems, appliances, office equipment, and other programmable devices.

Forensic Science

The precise date of when forensic science began is unclear as there are many different fields in which forensic science can be applied. Certainly, people have been trying to determine how people died for thousands of years. In the Chinese book *Hsi Duan Yu* (*The Washing Away of Wrongs*), which appeared about 1248, the author details methods to distinguish the effects of different ways of dying, for example, death by drowning as opposed to death by strangulation (Kind and Overman, 1972). Nearly 700 years later, the first crime laboratory was established in the United States by the Los

Angeles Sheriff Department in 1930 (De Forest, Gaensslen, and Lee, 1983). Howard Schmidt, who served as an advisor to President George W. Bush and President Barack Obama, is credited with establishing the first U.S. government digital forensics laboratory (Defense News, 2010). Although forensic science has been evolving for many centuries, digital forensics is a relatively new development.

For something to be considered a science, it has to study, describe, and investigate phenomena in its field. A key aspect of this is that new knowledge generated by the study and investigation has to be repeatable. A peer review process is often followed, including within a lab and the publication process. A complex investigation can have many opportunities for error or misinterpretation, and the review process helps reduce the instances of error. In the digital forensics field, tools and techniques are often reviewed, but it is not uncommon for the findings that are presented in court cases to be the work of a single investigator and therefore unverified. In many situations, digital forensics does not have a scientific rigor behind it, which is present in other forensic areas such as wet labs. Part of the reason is that digital forensics is a relatively new science, and another reason is that digital technology progresses at such a rapid rate that the digital forensic processes tend to lag the pace of technological innovation. Figure 1.1 is a flowchart representation of the scientific process.

There are three aspects of the scientific process that I want to highlight. The first is to clearly define the question or purpose of the research. The second is to define a hypothesis. A hypothesis is a potential explanation for a phenomenon. A digital

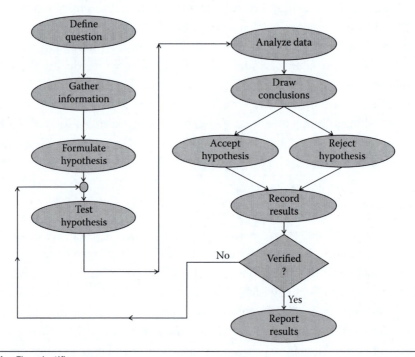

Figure 1.1   The scientific process.

forensic investigator often needs to develop a hypothesis to explain what happened on a computer and what it was used for. The third aspect that I want to emphasize is that many discussions of the scientific process overlook verification of results. Too often this is not done, and improper results are reported. Digital forensic cases can be life changing for many individuals, and every effort must be taken to ensure that the findings of the investigation are accurate. I do not want to discount the other steps in the scientific process, but I wanted to emphasize those three aspects—and in particular, verification of results.

Digital forensics is not limited to criminal investigation. It can be used to solve problems in a corporate setting such as recovering lost files and reconstructing information from damaged equipment and also to test for changes to devices that are subject to a stimulus. Malware and botnet research are other areas that use digital forensics, particularly when trying to determine impacts. An example would be to use forensic processes to establish the baseline state of a device, introduce the stimulus, and then compare the resulting state with the baseline.

What Does It Take to Be a Digital Forensic Investigator?

Digital forensic investigators need skills and interests in a variety of areas. The first question I ask someone who is considering this field is if they like puzzles. When investigating a case, you may not know any details other than that something has happened. So if someone needs to be shown or told what has occurred, they may not be a good fit for this field. Sometimes, cases come to an investigator's attention with instructions to find out what the computer or device user was doing. At times this may be an open request, whereas other times it is within a specific time frame.

Many cases follow a similar pattern, and a methodology similar to that outlined in Chapter 2 can help with a consistent investigation. However, many times the investigator needs to improvise an approach as there is not always a clear way to do things. This can be the result of new technology in which a methodology has not been developed, due to cost issues, or simply because it is the first time the investigator has encountered that situation. The point is that an investigator needs to be someone who can figure things out, not rely solely on others to do so. Another important characteristic is the ability to handle frustration because investigative tools and software do not always function without their challenges. This can be a fairly common occurrence when dealing with cell phones and small devices. I have had many students who stop their investigation in class at the first sign of difficulty rather than working through the challenges. They do not even try to find insight into their difficulty through the web or help system provided with the tool. Someone needs to be persistent and creative to be a successful investigator.

Another critical aspect of being a forensic investigator is the ability to keep your mouth closed. Case specifics usually require some level of confidentiality, and this must be maintained. Similarly, if someone is looking to enter the field as a private investigator or law enforcement professional, lack of a criminal record may be mandatory. Within a corporate setting, investigators may not need to be licensed, but they do need to maintain a high degree of integrity within the context of the corporation. I have gone through many smartphones and computers covertly to determine the degree of an employee's misconduct. The result is that I know what personnel changes are likely to occur before anyone else.

Irrespective of whether the environment is corporate, law enforcement, or as a private investigator, a background check is likely to occur. Particularly, in law enforcement and private investigator licensing, fingerprint registration is likely a requirement. Private investigators also need bonding and/or liability insurance. Most states require that private investigators have experience before becoming licensed, so students who are fresh out of college may find that they need to work for someone else under their license before becoming individually licensed.

The work itself seems to follow a sine wave rather than a consistent flow. Cases often explode into multiple devices and locations, which can mean long and inconsistent hours. After-hours investigation may be the rule for some cases, and often this may be at a distant site. What does seem to be the rule is that cases appear when they are not expected, and it is good practice to be ready. For example, computer forensics investigations usually include taking forensic images of the computers under investigation. Typically, this means taking a forensic image of the storage devices. The location where the images are being copied to should be forensically prepared in advance. For example, if a computer has a 1-TB hard drive, the forensic image could be taken on another 1-TB hard drive. This forensic image hard drive should not just be a new hard drive that is in an unopened box from a retail store because it is unknown what may already be stored on that drive. New hard drives commonly come with utilities and other programs preinstalled. A hard drive should be completely erased and reformatted before it is used. Experienced investigators often wipe a hard drive and then overwrite the entire drive with a hex character. This process takes time, and when time is of the essence, preparing forensic storage media in advance can save considerable time.

The forensic process is discussed later in the book, including Chapter 2, but let us complete the thought on forensically prepared storage media. The purpose of forensically prepared storage media is that it allows the investigator to testify that the only information contained on the forensic image drive is the one from the suspect computer and that there is no evidence of contamination. Anything that is not part of the forensic image would be the hex character that was due to the wiping process. Hash algorithms, such as MD5 and SHA-1, are also used to verify that an exact copy has been taken.

Educational Opportunities

Education is necessary to become competent in any profession, and digital forensics is no exception. Education can take many forms including university instruction, attendance at conferences, vendor classes, workshops, and self-study. Each of these should be evaluated to determine if it helps move someone toward their educational goal. College and university educational opportunities can be evaluated in a number of ways such as asking previous students and those affiliated with the courses and programs. Several designations and accreditation levels can help determine the maturity of the offerings. For example, the National Security Agency (NSA) has a center of academic excellence accreditation that is rigorous and appropriate. There are several levels to this designation, so inquiry into which level has been attained is good due diligence. An additional factor would be to inquire regarding the experience of the faculty. Other questions include the following: Do the faculty actively research and/or consult in digital forensics? Are they licensed and/or certified as investigators? How many cases have they investigated? What tools and technologies will the student be exposed to? How large are the classes and do they have a hands-on component? How long has the institution been offering courses?

Vendor classes focus on tools that they provide, although instructors will often provide insight into complimentary tools and techniques that are not part of the vendor's products. Some of these classes are offered online, which provides convenience in logistics and can help minimize costs. Commercial products can be expensive, and there may be other tools that also need to be purchased, so it is important to have an overall budget in place. Vendors may also sponsor their own conference and/or participate in other conferences. Conferences are a good way to develop a feel for how well products are received and what other things need to be considered.

SANS Institute provides very good education and training that is not tool specific. It offers intensive-focused instruction on specific topics that can lead to well-recognized and respected certifications. There are other similar organizations, but I have had two colleagues who have attended the SANS Institute and they gave it very high marks.

Self-study is an inexpensive way to develop skills, but it does require a large-time commitment. Personally, I think that self-study is the first step in the education process for a field like digital forensics. You can get a reasonable feel for the field and lay a foundation for a more advanced study at conferences, universities, and workshops. It is a very uncomfortable feeling to attend an educational opportunity without a foundation. The resulting insecurity may not allow you for maximizing the experience because of information overload or a simple misunderstanding that could have been avoided with preliminary self-study.

What Opportunities Are There for Digital Forensic Investigators?

Some of the more common areas for digital forensics investigators would be in law enforcement, the federal government, corporations, and as a private investigator. Typical law enforcement positions would be as a detective and/or in a crime lab, but some agencies deploy low-level forensic tools more broadly throughout the organization. Corrections personnel may also use forensic techniques to ensure that parole conditions are being adhered to. A large portion of the focus of law enforcement digital forensic efforts include child exploitation and sexually abusive material. Cell phone analysis is also a very significant component of the law enforcement efforts.

Federal government positions may reside within agencies such as the CIA, FBI, Secret Service, ATF, and Department of Defense. An area that uses digital forensics extensively that most people do not realize is the Postmaster General. The Department of Homeland Security is an agency that contracts services more often than some of the other cabinet level agencies, and digital forensics fits into this arrangement. Various agencies and departments handle things differently. For example, one location may be a general digital forensics lab, whereas another may maintain a higher level of expertise. Some locations may specialize in certain types of forensic activity, and some agencies may have multiple levels of expertise.

A federal agency that has a significant digital forensics presence is the NSA, which is one of the top organizations in the world in digital forensics and associated technologies. People who are interested in working for the NSA should consider attending a university that has been designated a NSA center of excellence. Preference is often given for positions, internships, and scholarships for the students who graduate from these centers of excellence.

Corporate positions in digital forensics can vary considerably in terms of responsibilities and focus. An individual may focus on data recovery of damaged or deleted files, investigation of security breaches, and investigation of employees who recently left the organization to find out what they were doing in the days leading up to leaving the company. Part of the reason for this type of investigation may be to see if the individual engaged in inappropriate activities such as copying sensitive information. Other responsibilities may include fraud investigation, employee misconduct, and research and development. Particularly, for law firms, forensic investigators may be involved in electronic discovery (e-discovery). E-discovery uses forensic tools to search through computers, networks, and storage devices in the discovery phase of a law suit. Simply looking for file names is not sufficient as the sought-after-documents may be e-mail or perhaps there is a question if the information even exists. E-discovery tools crawl through computers, networks, and storage media not unlike a search engine crawls through the World Wide Web. However, the e-discovery tools crawl to search for various keywords as opposed to a search engine that indexes everything that it finds.

Private investigators may be self-employed or work for a larger organization or law firm. The tools and technologies involved in digital forensics can be quite expensive, which may lead to concentrating in various subfields. For example, cell phone forensic tools can approach a purchase price of $10,000 with an annual maintenance fee of a few thousand dollars. Usually, investigators need multiple tools, so a reasonably equipped cell phone forensic investigator may invest $25,000 into tools in addition to training and other ongoing expenses. Computer forensics can involve a similar expense, and this does not include some of more advanced situations such as password and encryption cracking technologies.

What Are the Trends and Challenges in Digital Forensics?

One trend that is occurring is standardization and licensing of forensic investigators. In several states, it is a felony to perform digital forensic services without being licensed as a private investigator. The requirements for licensure vary, so the appropriate state agency should be consulted. It is important that individuals understand how the state within which they reside defines digital forensics so that they do not find themselves in a legal situation.

A recent study that I conducted of Michigan law enforcement (Gogolin, 2010) indicated a rapid increase in the number of cases requiring digital forensic services and a significant shortage of forensic investigators. It appears that if most criminal cases do not already have a digital aspect that they will in the near future. Surveillance devices and the prevalence of things such as cell phones are one of the main reasons for the rise in digital aspects. Social media, where planning and bragging of exploits occurs, almost guarantees that there will be digital artifacts.

Cell phone and mobile device ownership and usage surpassed 5 billion in 2010 (BBC News, 2010). This provides for the capture of information with embedded devices such as cameras, as well as for the exchange of information verbally and through technologies such as text messaging and e-mail. The integration of smartphones into the World Wide Web and social media provides for a rich and extensive number of artifacts that may be of interest to a digital forensic investigator.

Most cell phones and camera-equipped mobile devices have GPS capabilities. This allows the camera to incorporate the GPS coordinates of the location where a picture was taken into the picture file header. The analysis of pictures and videos, whether from cell phones or surveillance systems, is an explosive growth area. The images often need to be enhanced to obtain the necessary level of detail, and this expertise with graphics is a skill that requires a combination of training and technology that is not commonly available.

The movement toward a cloud environment is changing the digital forensics world. Cloud computing uses computing and storage resources from a pool. The pooled resources may be contracted from a third-party cloud provider. The third party often shares the pooled resources among many organizations. A key advantage of cloud architecture is that if a contracting organization needs extra resources for a short period they can contract the resources from the cloud provider. When they no longer need the resources, they simply revert to smaller amount of resources. This saves the organization money by eliminating the need to purchase equipment that they only need for a short period.

Cloud computing is kind of like a food catering service. If you want to throw a big party, it makes sense to rent seating and rather than buy several tables and chairs that you will not need after the party. When the party is over, the seating is cleaned and goes back to the owner, who then is free to rent it out to someone else who needs it. When the next renter receives the seating, it is in a clean state and there is no evidence that you had the seating. This illustrates the challenge with cloud computing for a forensic investigator. When you no longer need the resources that are contracted, the resource is contracted for another purpose. This can create multiple situations of interest in terms of forensics.

Scenario 1: If the data on the cloud storage device is deleted but not wiped when it is repurposed, there is potential for reconstruction of and access to the data that was previously on the device by someone who should not have access.

Scenario 2: If the data on the cloud storage is deleted and wiped when it is repurposed, recovery of the data or artifacts is not possible—especially if the storage resource is already in use by another entity.

The cloud environment also means that artifacts may no longer be contained on a single device, which can complicate discovering where the artifact originated. The very nature of the cloud, where resources can be used for a short time and then repurposed, means that artifacts can exist one moment and then disappear the next. Someone perpetrating a crime could contract cloud resources similar to what was previously outlined in scenario 2. Once the perpetrator is finished with the resources, the evidence is wiped and the resources are used by someone else, likely completely destroying the evidence trail. This type of situation has actually been occurring for many years in the form of botnets and similar technologies. The advances in cloud computing allow taking nefarious activity to a whole new level, which makes advancements in forensics that much more critical.

Anti-forensics, which is covered in Chapter 11, is attempting to hide, destroy, or alter artifacts to prevent their reconstruction by forensic analysis. Using anti-forensic techniques can make forensic reconstruction difficult or even impossible. Many tools are created to provide security for individuals who use intense algorithms and techniques. There is little to prevent the use of these tools in activities of less-than-honorable intent, which may frustrate forensic efforts. Even when methods have been developed to address these tools, the time and computer processing power required to defeat the tools and techniques are often prohibitive.

Another aspect that is not so much a trend but rather evidence that the world is becoming a smaller place is the internationalization that is enabled through the ease of connectivity. The language and cultural implications, as well as the ability of criminal perpetrators to be in different countries at the time of their transgressions, give rise to a multitude of challenges for investigators. Very few technical degree programs require foreign language fluency, which can hamstring an investigation from the start. Foreign languages and dialects present a number of challenges in understanding communication such as e-mail, as well as the extra difficulty that slang and idiomatic expressions introduce. In part, due to the proliferation of digital devices and Internet use and network connectivity, these challenges will likely only increase.

The worldwide nature of connectivity presents other challenges. There are jurisdictional and cooperation issues to deal with. Even within the United States, a case can be interpreted as a felony in one county but interpreted as a misdemeanor in another. State lines have not even been crossed! Crimes that cross state lines or international borders can be much more difficult to address. Perpetrators know which countries are likely to cooperate in a situation and plan accordingly. Servers are often hosted in countries that have lax laws and/or enforcement against a particular activity. Illegal online gambling servers are commonly hosted in Latin American countries (Menn, 2010).

To complicate things even further, the location of servers can quickly change with the use of virtual technology. Virtualization allows one physical computer to run multiple logical computers within it. A rough example is when someone sets up multiple accounts on their home personal computer. Little Johnny signs on to his account, with his own screen background and configuration characteristics. Stephanie signs on to the same computer using her account and uses her own configuration that is independent of Little Johnny's. Virtualization takes this farther in that the operating system can be installed multiple times in different locations on one computer, and the multiple installations can be run simultaneously and independently. Virtualization has existed in a corporate computer environment for decades, but recent advancements have reduced the cost and complexity so that it can be used by a very broad range of individuals. These virtualization capabilities help support the movement to a cloud architecture. An individual can create a virtual machine and potentially move or copy it between computers—and countries—within minutes. The implications of this in a digital forensics environment are dramatic.

Computer forensics often focuses on storage media such as a computer hard drive. Hard drives are rapidly increasing in capacity, and other storage technologies are evolving. Flash memory and solid state drives (SSD) are likely to replace hard drives in the near future because of their superior access speeds. Bell and Boddington (2010) found that SSD can confound current digital forensic techniques. Similarly, Wei et al. (2011) found that traditional hard drive sanitation techniques are ineffective on SSD. Computer technology will continue to evolve, and these examples illustrate that a forensic examiner must evolve as the paradigms within which they operate evolve.

The last trend that I want to discuss—although there are many more that could be touched on—is simply the explosion of data and storage capabilities. An individual can purchase a terabyte of hard drive storage for less than $50. This puts the ability to store multiple terabytes of data within the reach of an incredible number of people. It also means that corporations can create dramatically large databases and data warehouses that were previously inconceivable. It can take days to perform a keyword search on a 1-TB hard drive using forensic tools. Extrapolate that out to a corporate environment where the storage capacity is far greater, and it is possible to find that it is impossible to keyword searches on all of the storage media using current techniques. One challenge is that it may not be able to "freeze" all of the data in all the systems at the current state. Data is always changing and being modified by multiple systems and users. It is kind of like telling the world to stop rotating while measurements are taken. Further, the data may reside in many locations. The point is that digital forensics is a far different environment in a corporate setting than it is when looking at an individual's private computer. But with the advancements in computer technology, some of the challenges with corporate digital forensics are appearing in the environment of an individual's private computer.

Resources Available to Digital Forensic Investigators

Before I describe some of the tools and technologies, I would like to describe some of the organizations and other resources that are available. Formal training is one of the most important considerations. In a legal situation such as a court case, competency of an investigator is going to be one of the first things evaluated. If the investigator has little or no current relevant training or certification, the outcome of the case may be in doubt. Most vendors provide training on their tools, and many conferences and information security organizations provide training opportunities.

Online resources in many instances are the most valuable. Knowledge bases and virtual communities can be invaluable in working through problems that an investigator encounters. Vendors often provide a searchable bulletin board that is frequented by users of the vendor's products. Open-source tools often have very passionate support groups. Social networks can be valuable in obtaining contacts that may help provide insight into issues. Organizations such as the International Information Systems Security Certification Consortium (ISC²) provide training, testing, and certification in the areas that compliment digital forensics. The federal government has a variety of programs such as InfraGard and opportunities through the Department of Homeland Security that can be very beneficial. Search.org is one of many organizations that I have found that provide free online resources that I frequently take advantage of.

Many universities have research groups that specialize in digital forensics that may be willing to help. Which university or research group is appropriate to consult depends on the type of the case or situation the investigator is working on. For example, if the case involves incident response, Carnegie Mellon's CERT could prove to be a valuable resource. But if the incident is something recovery of data from damaged media, contacting a different university may be appropriate. It is also important to realize that top research universities are not the only game in town. Researchers at smaller universities may actually have broader exposure and more field experience than those at universities where research is a primary goal. A good way to wade through the maze is to find a third-party reference such as the NSA. The NSA designates universities as centers of excellence if they meet certain criteria, and most universities that have a significant presence in digital forensics have gone through this certification process. Additionally, the NSA certification is in different areas, so this can further assist finding potential resources.

Many tools and technologies are available to assist forensic examiners in addressing the challenges described earlier. Chapter 3 includes a discussion of tools and techniques, as well as how they fit into the overall scheme of a digital forensics investigation. There are commercially available tools as well as open source. Some tools are very specialized and focus on doing one particular thing well, whereas other tools attempt to address a much broader perspective. There is often a leapfrog situation occurring where a new version of a particular tool surpasses its competitors. A short time later a competitor may introduce a new version and it becomes the leader until the next leapfrog situation. For that reason, I will not try to rank particular tools and technologies or provide detailed instructions on how to perform a specific operation with a tool. However, I am a firm believer in leaving bread crumbs for myself and anyone else to follow. So I will not hesitate to describe my experiences with tools. It is my hope that I can point out the potholes that I have encountered so that you can avoid them or at least prepare for them.

Conclusion

Digital forensics is a rapidly advancing field that has many challenges and crosswinds. The opportunities are endless, but they are not for the faint of heart. Frustration is a common partner, so the ability and mentality to press on through is a key characteristic an investigator should have. Someone who needs to be shown how to do everything may want to rethink their career options. A can-do attitude is essential, but the investigator does not need to go it alone. A variety of resources are available to assist, and most of the investigators who have worked through the learning curve to achieve competence are more than eager to help others do the same. Usually, they had others to lean on, so once you reach a level of expertise with the assistance of others, do not forget to return the favor.

References

BBC News. (2010). Over 5 Billion Mobile Phone Connections Worldwide. Retrieved on July 2, 2011 from http://www.bbc.co.uk/news/10569081.

Bell, G., and Boddington, R. (2010). Solid State Drives: The Beginning of the End for Current Practice in Digital Forensic Recovery? *The Journal of Digital Forensics, Security and Law*, Vol 5(3).

De Forest, P. R., Gaensslen, R. E., and Lee, H. C. (1983). *Forensic Science: An Introduction to Criminalistics*, McGraw-Hill, New York.

Defense News. (2010). An Online 'War'? Retrieved on June 20, 2011 from http://www.defensenews.com/story.php?i=4567292&c=FEA&s=COM.

Gogolin, G. (2010). The Digital Crime Tsunami. *Digital Investigation*, Vol. 7(1-2).

Kind, S., and Overman, M. (1972). *Science against Crime*, Aldus Books, London, UK.

Menn, J. (2010). Fatal System Error: The Hunt for the New Crime Lords Who Are Bringing Down the Internet, PublicAffairs, New York.

Wei, M., Grupp, L., Spada, F., and Swanson, S. (2011). Reliably Erasing Data from Flash-Based Solid State Drives. Usenix Fast 11 Conference on File and Storage Technologies, San Jose, CA.

2

DIGITAL FORENSIC APPROACHES AND BEST PRACTICES

Introduction

Forensics is the application of the scientific process to answer a question. For digital forensics to be an accepted science, it has to apply the scientific method. The scientific method is the application of a set of accepted and verifiable steps to investigate a question or problem. The digital forensic process needs to include a thorough enough review to confirm findings, and it should not overlook artifacts that may discredit the findings. In other words, the investigator needs to follow due diligence and review all facts, not just the facts that produce a desired result. In many instances, the forensic review will be performed for one party and the same evidence will undergo a similar review for an opposing party. If the investigator produces inaccurate results, this will likely surface when the results from the two opposing parties come together in court or some other forum. One method to help solidify results is to have a second set of eyes review the results before they are finalized. Similarly, the forensic results from the opposing team should be reviewed by you to verify the results. As Ronald Reagan used to say, "Doveryai, no proveryai," or "Trust but verify."

There is more than one way to approach a case from a forensic investigation perspective. The circumstances surrounding the investigation impact how the investigation is conducted. For example, there are differences between corporate, civil, and criminal situations. There may be time constraints that impact the speed at which an investigation can occur, emerging technology may be involved, media may be damaged, or perhaps the operation has covert requirements. So to say an investigation should always follow a prescribed methodology may not be accurate. However, there are still some basic elements that every effort should be made in order to maintain. Among these are do not contaminate the evidence, be objective, present the facts, and give a best effort.

There are situations where all you need to do is to verify the presence or absence of something on a device. For example, I know a forensic investigator who works for corrections that deals with people on parole. He frequently does a field exam of the cell phone or the computer. Because of the volume of cases that he deals with, he has time only to look for something specific, not go on a fishing expedition.

In many situations, the digital forensic exam supports a larger case issue. Since the digital piece is just a portion of the overall case, often times the forensic exam receives a corresponding amount of attention. If the case is likely to be plea bargained, minimal forensic effort may be expended until or unless the case goes to court. Figure 2.1 shows the crimes reported to the Internet Crime Complaint Center up to 2009, with projections to 2020. It clearly depicts the challenge that digital forensic investigators face in terms of sheer volume of potential case work.

A corporate investigation may center on the presence or absence of a particular file or set of files, software, or correspondence. I have worked on cases where the purpose was to determine who was involved in a particular scheme. It was not criminal, but more on the order of misuse of corporate assets. In a situation such as this, the convicting evidence may be on a server or a device belonging to someone other than the target of the investigation. In this case that I am referring to, an employee chose to leave the employment of an organization. A cursory review of one of the corporate-issued devices contained communication between several individuals who detailed potential misuse of corporate resources. The computers and devices of the individuals in the correspondence were examined for further detail with regard to the resource misuse. Information was found by conducting keyword searches on information in the original communication and the employees were terminated. This was a targeted search, not a comprehensive investigation.

The point that I have been trying to make is that the methodology one follows in a digital forensic investigation depends on the circumstance. In court proceedings, this concept can make or break a case. It is important to know why you did things in an investigation, but it is also important to know why you did not do things in an investigation. Additionally, it is important to know the impact of those decisions. I will describe common steps in a forensic exam, the reasons for doing them, and try to give a sense for their relative importance. Realize that technology evolves rapidly and that this should be used as a guideline.

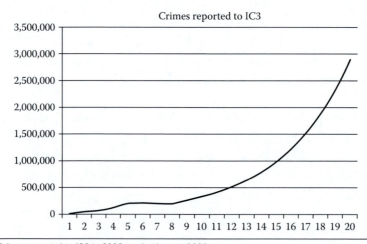

Figure 2.1   Crimes reported to IC3 to 2009, projections to 2020.

There are agencies and organizations that provide outlines for specific purposes. The American Chief Police Officers publishes a good practice guide (ACPO, 2011). Within this guide are four principles:

Principle 1: No action taken by law enforcement agencies or their agents should change data held on a computer or storage media, which may subsequently be relied upon in court.

Principle 2: In circumstances where a person finds it necessary to access original data held on a computer or on storage media, that person must be competent to do so and be able to give evidence explaining the relevance and the implications for their actions.

Principle 3: An audit trail or other record of all processes applied to computer-based electronic evidence should be created and preserved. An independent third party should be able to examine those processes and achieve the same result.

Principle 4: The person in charge of the investigation (the case officer) has overall responsibility for ensuring that the law and these principles are adhered to.

Another organization that provides guidance with forensics is the National Institute of Standards and Technology. They have created several documents that deal with digital forensics, including NISTR 7250, NISTR 7490, and SP800-10 for cell phone forensics.

These guidelines have a lot of good information and considerations for performing forensic examinations. The guidelines tend to follow behind the advances in technology and forensic practice, so it is not uncommon for an examiner to feel a bit like Captain Kirk in that they may need to boldly go where no one has gone before.

First Response

Interviews should be at the top of the list when responding to a situation and beginning an investigation. The interview may be with coworkers who have knowledge of the case, suspects, or victims. All too often, a computer or a device is turned over to an investigator for an investigation and no clear purpose is provided. People seem to think that an investigator can magically figure out what needs to be done. There have been many cases where I have been working on a case and someone "remembers" that they forgot to tell me the key information. For a digital forensic investigator, interview questions should frame the type of investigation that needs to be performed—incident response, child exploitation, civil, and so on. Think about the types of keywords that would be useful—e-mail addresses, names, locations, phone numbers, account numbers, and other things that will generate information, which will be useful in the case. It should go without saying that information from an interview should be written down and dated. Potentially, the interview may become part of the final forensic report.

The equipment that you bring to process a scene should be on a list. If you find that something you need is not on the list, add it to your list so that you have it the next time. You do not need everything on the list at every scene, but reviewing the list before responding to a case is a good sanity check before going out. I like to store things in the same location and order in a closet so that I kind of visually check things as I load them up to deploy.

Before you go to a site, make sure that you have authority to do so. Written documentation is preferred. If you are in a covert situation, it may make sense to tip-off local law enforcement that you will be removing equipment from a business in the middle of the night. Whether it is related to law enforcement (search warrant) or, make sure that the documentation is broad enough that you can take manuals and notebooks that are in the vicinity. Notebooks may have passwords or other information that can help with a difficult case. A general list of items that may be necessary in a response situation is as follows:

1. *Response computer*. A portable that is in a Pelican® case protects it when it gets knocked around and exposed to the elements. Make sure the manuals are loaded.
2. *Dongles*. You do not want to get to a location and be unable to preview a device or activate the software.
3. *Smartphone or other device with Internet access*. The forensic computer is often not equipped to access the Internet so that it can be free of outside influences. A smartphone or other device has web access so that you can access manuals and vendor websites for technical support. Some 12-year-old kid probably made a YouTube video that shows how to pull a hard drive from a device that you are unfamiliar with.
4. *Imaging devices*. Examples would be things like an Atola Imager®, Ninja Forensic®, and DeepSpar Imager®. For field work, the Ninja is one of my favorite tools because it does not require a computer to operate. These kinds of tools make images far faster than through a computer or a USB interface and serve other purposes such as strong wiping of media and recovery of data from a damaged media.
5. *Extension cords and power strips*. I prefer a separate extension cord and power strip because if you only need the power strip, you do not need an extra cord to deal with. First response often takes place in a stressful environment, so place where they would not be a tripping hazard.
6. *Camera*. A good resolution digital camera is fine. For more advanced situations, consider a digital single-lens reflex (DSLR) with a macro or close-up lens. For some situations, you may need a small tent or shield to help with light and reflective glare—particularly with phones and small devices.
7. *Paper, pen, pencil*. When I worked in a grocery store in high school, the produce manager told me that your best friend is your pencil. Write it down.

8. *Labels and indelible ink pen such as a Sharpie®.* You want something that writes in most environments and would not smear or erase. Color coding can be helpful.

9. *Cell phone with contact list.* The contact list should include forensic vendors, people who may be able to provide assistance if you encounter something difficult, unusual, or time-consuming.

10. *Food and beverages.* You almost never read about this, but digital forensics can be time-consuming. Calling in a pizza usually is not appropriate or an option.

11. *Rags.* Dust and dirt can be key evidence, so photograph it. Computers and cables can be quite dirty and you may need to clean something up.

12. *Change of clothes.* You may get dirty crawling around under desks or other places. I have soaked a shirt just from the stress of a situation, and there are a number of times where you will appreciate a fresh set of clothes.

13. *Latex (or similar) exam gloves.* There are some things you do not want to touch or perhaps leave fingerprints on.

14. *Black light.* For detecting proteins. One of the main reasons you may want the exam gloves.

15. *Tool kit.* This should include micro screwdrivers like you would use for eyeglasses all the way up to full size. At the minimum, it should include electrical tape, duct tape, electrical zip ties, razor blades, pliers, screws, and bolts. A driver with torx heads—particularly #6 and #8—and other irregular heads also come in handy.

16. *First aid kit.* The inside of computers can be sharp.

17. *Network cables, hub, crossover cables, IDE/SATA adapters, and USB to multiple interface adapter.*

18. *Boot disks.* These should include things like Helix, Linen, Winen, and Windows password reset utilities.

19. *Blank CD-ROMs and DVDs.*

20. *Grounding mechanism.* These often come with computer tool kits. The purpose is to prevent static charge damage to components.

21. *Write blockers.* These should include USB, IDE, SATA, and SCSI capabilities. Carry more than one type as sometimes device recognition firmware can be flacky and it helps to have options. I also have a yellow read or write blocker that can be useful if you need to improvise something in the field.

22. *Hard drives.* They should be wiped before arriving on scene. Most hard drives tend to have utilities and other things preloaded. Completely wipe them and format them with an appropriate file system so that they are ready for use. Never throw away the plastic bags in which new hard drives come in. Use them for static protection during transport and storage for both target and suspect hard drives. Consideration points: capacity, external drive, ATA, SATA, Solid State, and laptop/desktop/server.

23. *Flash drives.* These are handy for phone acquisition for tools such as Cellebrite, as well as targeted acquisitions from computers.
24. *Flash drive equipped for RAM acquisition.* The file system you format the flash drive may impact the type of computer you can acquire from.
25. *Mobile device equipment.* This would include tools such as Cellebrite or XRY, as well as Faraday bags and battery-powered trickle charger.
26. *Headlight and flashlight.* I have found that wearing a headlight is much more convenient than holding a flashlight, particularly when you are under a desk or in a nighttime situation.
27. *Empty backpacks, bags, and other carrying devices.* Make sure you have a way to transport the equipment that you will be acquiring.
28. *Tape.* Tape has many uses including serving as labels. I like masking tape as it does not leave a sticky residue that is common with duct tape.
29. *String.* More for improvising unforeseen things.
30. *Scissors and wire cutters.* Sometimes things are taped or wired together and you need to break the bond.
31. *Magnifying glass.* This has many uses including reading serial numbers on hard drives and labels on components.
32. *Blanket and pads.* Primarily for protection of equipment during transport, but also to serve as a barrier if you need to crawl on the floor.
33. *Securing straps.* These are to secure the equipment and components for transport. Seat belts can be useful for this purpose as well.
34. *Extra mouse and keyboard.* Some devices may have a touch interface that can prove awkward.
35. *Suction cups.* These have multiple uses including retrieval of a hard drive from an iMac.
36. *Soap, water, and hand sanitizer.* There is not always a place to wash up—yet there usually is a need.

When you arrive on a scene, you may be the only one present—or at least the only one with the requisite technical skills. I worked with a colleague who was indoctrinated with the military's OODA approach: Observer, Orient, Decide, and Act. This means that you need to observe the situation, orient yourself to the environment, decide on a course of action, and then execute the course of action. The colleague explained that he read about an experienced forensic investigator who indicated that his first course of action when sitting down at the keyboard of a computer that may contain digital evidence was to sit on his hands. This forced him into the OODA cycle.

A wet laboratory (biological) forensic analyst would not want someone walking through a crime scene or handling evidences indiscriminately. Doing so may render the potential evidence useless. Similarly, if someone logs on to a digital device and starts going through logs or other things on the device, they may complicate or compromise the investigation. Once again, the situation impacts the action cycle.

In a criminal case, preserving the evidence may be at odds with what the owner of the device wants to do. In a business setting, the owner of the device may be the owner of the business, so commonality of purpose is likely to be more consistent. However, the way to accomplish the goal may be at odds. A forensic investigator may want to shut down a machine, whereas doing so may reduce the ability of the business to function. Understanding and communicating the implications of this type of investigative decision point is a key aspect of the investigation.

Documenting the scene is an important consideration because it defines the environment and helps explain considerations made in the investigation. Documenting can be done by diagram, written text, pictures, and video. Personally, I rely on diagramming, text, and pictures and seldom use video. Video can be good in that it can be self-documenting, but it is difficult to utilize when responding individually to a situation. When working alone, it is a challenge to have video camera presence, have proper resolution, and stay in frame. Talking aloud may prove useful in this situation. But to utilize video effectively, it needs to be someone's main function. If there are multiple responders to a scene, even a dedicated video photographer may be challenged to accurately depict the scene.

There are numerous bag and tag checklists available on the web from government sources such as the Department of Homeland Security. Rather than create another checklist, I will simply refer you to those sources. The URLs tend to change, so Google is your friend. One thing that is not on the checklists is some of the peripheral things such as inventory. Inventory everything you bring to a scene and everything you remove from a scene. It is helpful to tag every item with a keyed label rather than just listing it on a sheet of paper as a hard drive. Instead, break it down using things like serial numbers and places of origin and match them to photograph number(s) taken on scene.

One of the most important decisions during first response is how to deal with a live system. This applies to mobile devices, computers, and other components. The live memory (often referred to as physical memory or RAM) may contain passwords, IP addresses, active processes, and other things that can be very useful in an investigation. Encrypted volumes may be in an unencrypted state when mounted to a live system, which provides access to otherwise encrypted data. This capability can be lost if the encrypted volume password is unknown and the computer were to be powered down.

Live system memory can be captured with a variety of tools. A common way is to load the memory acquisition tool onto a USB device. For a personal computer, obtaining a copy of what is in the live memory can be as simple as inserting the USB drive into the computer, bringing up a command line, and executing a small program from the USB drive to copy the contents of RAM to the USB device. This does modify a small portion of RAM, but the vast majority stays intact. For a Macintosh computer, the process is similar, but the USB drive should be formatted with a file system that is compatible. Computers come with a lot of RAM these days, so the

USB device should have a large capacity. While a Macintosh may be able to read from an NTFS files system, it cannot write to NTFS by default. So you may be out of luck if you show up on scene with a USB drive that is formatted with NTFS and your target computer is a Macintosh.

Responding to a live system in a corporate environment can present even larger challenges. For security reasons, servers may have USB disabled. This means that if you need to take an image of RAM, then using a USB device as outlined in the previous paragraph is not an option without changing the configuration settings to allow USB. Doing this changes the state of the computer, including some of the contents of RAM. It may also require a reboot, which completely defeats the purpose. Also, the amount of RAM on the computer may be many gigabytes, and so the USB device needs to have sufficient space.

Helix and commercial forensic tools are common techniques to acquire RAM. The challenge is what to do with the memory image after it is acquired as it is captured in an unformatted state. HBGary has a small footprint memory acquisition tool, which means that it impacts very little that resides in RAM. Additionally, HBGary has a memory formatting tool that is very useful in analysis. Remember, RAM can appear to be nothing more than a jumbled mess until it is analyzed with a memory analysis tool such as what HBGary provides.

Another situation that may occur in a corporate setting is virtualization. A server may be set up as a host that is running several virtual machines. The target of the investigation may be one of the virtual machines. Obtaining a copy of the contents of RAM can be difficult and may be further complicated if the host is running a different operating system than the virtual machines. One option may be to take a snapshot of the virtual machine, copy it to an external device, restore it in a laboratory, and then take a snapshot of RAM.

Mobile systems often require that they be live in order to perform a forensic exam. These devices are commonly password protected, and a device reset to original state may occur if the password is entered incorrectly a certain number of times. Therefore, it may be advantageous to maintain a mobile device in live state if that is how it was received. It is not a cut and dry decision though, as it can be a fairly simple process to remotely wipe a mobile device—particularly devices such as smartphones—thereby rendering the device useless to the investigation.

Responding to a Case

One of the challenges that an investigator faces is that they go to training and learn how to perform a variety of tasks, but they are usually stand-alone tasks that are tightly scripted within the context of the educational setting. Training classes tend to focus on a particular task, then they may be followed by an exercise. Then there are more task or exercise cycles until it is time for lunch or time to go home. Other training environments might be primarily lecture. Training that is not utilized within a short period of time is quickly lost. It seems like most of the training is forgotten after about a month, so if the investigator's first case does not occur shortly after the training, the ability to perform an investigation may be limited. Hopefully, there are other investigators who can help with the initial investigations.

When the investigator is faced with their first case after completing training, they might find themselves in a situation where they do not know where to begin or what techniques to employ. The purpose of this section is to outline common response methodology. Keep in mind that cases and their requirements can vary a great deal, so this is a guide—not gospel. Variables include whether it is a criminal, civil, corporate, or some other type of case. Other variables include the types of tools that will be used, the type of devices that will be examined, the time available for examination, and the budget. My standard tool set for responding to a computer incident is EnCase Forensic Edition, HBGary Responder, Tableau Write Blockers, Ninja Forensic Imager, forensically wiped target storage media, and tools and items from the response checklist found earlier in this chapter. My preference is to utilize internal drives as the target media (drive receiving the image) in the imaging process as I can often hook them up directly resulting in faster imaging, and they are cost-efficient relative to external drives. For the actual investigation process, my preference is to store the evidence and case information on an external drive such as a MyBook, because they provide a self-contained environment that can be easily accessed via USB and they tend to be more durable. Internal drives are not made to be connected and disconnected multiple times, whereas that is a design feature of an external drive. Additionally, external drives are easily stored and archived in a safe.

There are a number of scene-specific things to consider. First and foremost, ensure your safety. One time I performed a black bag job (off-hours acquisition) in a corporate environment that was part of a civil situation. The person being investigated appeared on scene while I was acquiring the evidence, even though there were protection orders in place. The individual left somewhat peacefully, but reappeared 10 minutes later. This was particularly stressful, because it is common to hear of someone who leaves a scene and then reappears a short time later with a weapon. Fortunately, there was no weapon, but stress levels were high.

The incident response itself should be planned and contingencies should be part of the plan. Figure 2.2 contains a guide that helps direct the response and examination process. It may not be possible to know what the configuration or capacity of the suspect devices are, and so come prepared with options and multiple forensically prepared storage devices. On occasion, a target drive may fail, so it is good to have spare drives available. The response may involve imaging multiple computers, so prioritize the order and plan ways to image multiple computes simultaneously, if necessary. The current metric that I use is being able to image and verify 80 gigabytes per hour using the Ninja Forensic. This can be extrapolated to estimate how much time the imaging process will consume. It will take longer to take an image using forensic software, particularly if the image is using USB connections.

EXAMINER:		
SUBJECT:		
COMPUTER MODEL/SN:		
EXPANSION CARDS:		
INTERNAL DRIVES:		
OPERATING SYSTEM:		
PRE-EXAMINATION	**TIME/DATE**	**NOTES:**
Review search auth/warrant; reports; statements		
Plan examination including equipment requirements		
Photograph evidence		
Examine media and secure components		
Register serial numbers, etc.		
Observe damaged, missing components		
Sign out evidence if it has already been secured		
EVIDENCE ACQUISITION		
Disconnect HDDs from power/check boot sequence		
Obtain date/time from CMOS, HDDs configuration		
Connect HDDs using write blocker technology		
Acquire evidence file with MD5 Hash		
Replace HDDs with original jumper settings		
Verify hash value and that there are zero errors		
Archive evidence files to server and check the file integrity		
Sign in/secure evidence		
EXAMINATION		
Recover Deleted Folders/Partitions on all drives/partitions		
Run File Mounter and create Logical Evidence File (LEF)		
Add LEF to case close mounted files to free RAM		
Signature Analysis Hash Analysis (Review Results)		
Email (Search Tab and webmail parser) results in records tab		
Peer to Peer search (Limewire and Kazaa Scripts)		
Index files not searchable by Encase and use Condition to search		
Conduct Keyword Search (Results in Search Hits)		
Gallery Viewer exam (not until after Signature Analysis)		
Movie file exam (Condition for Movies)		
Recycle Bin INFO2 record file Finder (ENSCRIPT)		
Internet History/Web Cache (Under Search Tab use comprehensive)		
Registry exam (Ntuser.dat, Sam, Security, System, Software)		

Figure 2.2   Forensic examination guide.

	TIME/DATE	NOTES:
Obtain time zone settings		
Windows—Recent, Print Spool, Sent To, Start Menu, EMF		
Windows—Favorites, Desktop, Temp		
.jpg/.gif/.emf/.bmp/.art Finder (Sweep CaseFile Finder EnScript)		
hyperfil.sys, pagefile		
Facebook/Social Networking searches		
Smartphone and mp3 player backups		
Chats: AOL IM, ICQ, Yahoo		
Additional scripts: Hotmail light script		
REPORT WRITING		
Write summary and signature page		
Organize evidence images, Hyperlink Report, Exam CD		
POST-EXAMINATION		
Write .cas file to final archive CD/DVD, EnCase version, Scripts		
Delete evidence images from Temp folders/wipe media		
NOTES:		HDD 0 JUMPER [: : : :]
		HDD 1 JUMPER [: : : :]
		HDD 2 JUMPER [: : : :]
		HDD 3 JUMPER [: : : :]
		OTHER JUMPER [: : : :]

Figure 2.2 (*Continued*) Forensic examination guide.

Once the response plan has been created and authorized, the scene should be secured as soon as the responders arrive on location. In a corporate environment, this may mean having security prevent access. In a law enforcement environment, this may involve coordination with other types of investigators. Bottom line is that if someone is not helping, then they should not be there. Diagram and photograph the scene. Photographs should be of multiple angles and attempt to take pictures that show how everything is connected to the computer. If you are taking the computer with you, label the cables and other devices so that they can be matched back to the computer. This is particularly important if multiple computers are being seized. Register the serial numbers and tags of all devices on an inventory sheet. Figure 2.3 is a sample of an inventory sheet. Secure the devices for transport and take them back to the laboratory. Look around for flash drives, printers, and other peripheral devices including manuals, CDs, and DVDs. Consider the environment during transport as you do not want to expose the devices to extremes in temperature. If a wide variation in temperature happens, allow the devices to reach room temperature before powering them on.

Computer Forensic Exam Notes				**CCU#**				
			Page 1 of 3					

Physical Exam								
CCU Item #	Requesting Agency Evidence Item #							
Brand Name	Model		Computer Type					
				Netbook	Tablet	Tower	Desktop	Laptop
Serial Number (if none include a unique number or markings)								
Color\Condition								
Hardware Capabilities **(circle the ones that the system has)**	VGA	PS2	USB	Firewire	Ethernet	CD DVD R RW	FDD	ZIP Drive
	DVI	Serial	Sound	Wireless	Modem	Smart Media	# of HDDs	Other
Media found in computer bays?								
BIOS Check (Detach HDDs)	System Date		Actual Date		System Time			Actual Time
Notes\Unusual Items:								

Hard Drive(s)	**Drive #1** (use columns if more than one)
Brand	
Model and or Size, Type (IDE, Sata)	
SN	
Notes (i.e. unattached, RAID suspected, jumper positions)	

Documentation of Lab Hardware and Software	
Forensic Drive Folder or location of case files	
Previewed Date and Physical Drive No.	
Software Used for Acquisition and for Analysis	
Acquired Date and Name given to Drive	
Write-Block Device Used	

Overview (Notes of bookmarked items and general impressions)	
Actual Physical Size of Drive	
List each volume's File System, Size and Type (OS, storage, backup recovery)	1)
Recovered Folders Check? File Signatures Check? Files Hashed? C4All Script used? Anti Virus Scan?	☐ ☐ ☐ ☐ ☐
Reviewed Directory Tree: Unique or Unusual Folders	
Review of Allocated Graphics Photoshop files or other unique graphic files? Scanned images? EXIF data?	Allocated

Figure 2.3 Computer forensics examination form.

Review of Movies	Allocated
Review of Unallocated Graphics, Lost, Orphaned, or Recovered from within files (i.e., Thumbs, Cache, Doc, Zips)	Unallocated
Review of Documents and Writings (i.e., file extensions) TXT WPS PDF WKS DOC XLS RTF CSV	Allocated Unallocated

Computer Forensic Exam Notes (*continued*)   **CCU#**

Page 2 of 3

Operating System Info

Operating System, Registered Owner\Organization, Install Date, Last Proper Shutdown, System File: Time Zone

User Name(s) in Registry, Computer Name, Attached Devices, Printers, Mapped or Network Drives

Detailed Analysis

Most Recent Time and Dates: What kind of files

Created

Accessed

Written

Modified

Timeline(s)

Activity surrounding (date/time)

Communication Programs: Screen names, Email addresses, Chats and Emails recovered, IEF results

Figure 2.3   (*Continued*) Computer forensics examination form.

Programs: (Document all programs using Encase Case Processor script) Anti virus, P2P, Photoshop, Remote Access (Logmein, GoToMyPC), Evidence Eliminator, Cleanup, Usenet, Internet Browsers
Log, System Files
Keyword Hits
Additional Notes

Computer Forensic Exam Notes (*continued*)   CCU#

Page 3 of 3

Review of Username _____ **(one page per user)**
(My) Documents, any authored items that tie a person with User name?
Unique Folders
(My) Pictures
(My) Video
(My) Music
Downloads
Recent
Desktop
Recycle Bin

Figure 2.3 (*Continued*) Computer forensics examination form.

Cookies

Program User Folders (i.e., Limewire Shared, My Received Files)

Internet Favorites

Internet History, Searches

Other/Notes

Completed by	Date

Digital Media Exam Notes	CCU#

Page 1 of 1

Physical Exam	
CCU Item #	Requesting Agency Evidence Item #
Item Type	Examiner Markings if any
Description	

Documentation of Lab Hardware and Software	
How was data preserved and protected from alteration?	Forensic Folder\Name given to evidence
Preview Date	Acquired Date	Forensic Software or Tools used (name, version, maker)

Overview (Notes of bookmarked items and general impressions)
Actual Physical Size

Volume(s): (Partition #, File System, Size and Type (Camera, Storage, etc.) If DVD/CD; Total Sessions?

Recovered Folders Check? File Signatures Check? Files Hashed? C4All Script used? Anti Virus Scan?	☐ ☐ ☐ ☐ ☐
Reviewed Directory Tree: Unique or Unusual Folders	

Figure 2.3 (*Continued*) Computer forensics examination form.

Review of Allocated Graphics Photoshop files or other unique graphic files? Scanned images? EXIF data?	Allocated
Review of Movies	Allocated

Review of Lost, Orphaned, Unallocated Graphics or
   Recovered from within files (i.e., Thumbs, Cache,
   Doc, Zips)
	Unallocated

Review of Documents and Writings (i.e., file extensions) TXT WPS PDF WKS DOC XLS RTF CSV	Allocated	Unallocated
Programs, Logs, System Files, Communications, Recycle Bin		

Completed by	**Date**
Forensic Exam Log	**CCU #**

Page of

Date	Name	Item #	Notes

Figure 2.3   (*Continued*) Computer forensics examination form.

There are many scenarios that an investigator may be faced with. Corporate settings may be handled different than a typical law enforcement setting. A single computer does not take as much logistical planning as multiple computers. There are also server, environment, and configuration considerations. The scenario we will work through is a single computer case that assumes an image of the suspect hard drive will be taken and then an investigation will ensue. Some forensic tools such as EnCase have preprogrammed scripts that can be run against an evidence file to "automatically" handle many of the aspects of an investigation. For the most part, this section reviews investigative concepts, not how a tool handles a particular aspect of forensic analysis.

Depending on the situation and case requirements, an investigator may preview a device to determine if taking an image is necessary. Imaging means making a verifiable bit for bit copy of the information on a device. Previewing means to review the potential evidence in a forensic state, but before imaging the evidence. If a computer is powered on, acquire an image of the RAM because there may be information such as passwords, bots, and viruses contained in RAM that could be helpful in an investigation. A decision point is to determine the likelihood of protection or destructive mechanisms on the computer. If the likelihood is high, a contingency plan should be made on how to image the computer. If the likelihood is low, power off the machine, disconnect and image the hard drive(s), connect them to write blockers and the investigation machine, and begin the imaging process. Some forensic tools include a software write blocker, in which case the physical write blockers are unnecessary. A specialized imaging tool could be used in place of using the write blockers and investigation machines. Both of these techniques are illustrated in Chapter 3.

It is critical that the hash values for the suspect computer and the image match and be documented. The hashes are usually expressed as MD5 and SHA1 values. The use of hashing is explained in more detail in Chapter 4. Good practice is to take a picture of the label on the suspect hard drive as a way to document the investigation. Serial numbers, storage capacity or sector count, and configuration are things that need to be recorded. The suspect computer should be booted and the BIOS checked for time zone settings. Establishing the time of when things occurred on the computer is central to many cases, and this can be one of the key pieces of evidence. In a corporate setting, computer clocks may be managed centrally, so this should be documented as well. The modified, accessed, created, and deleted times for the files on a computer help reconstruct events and activities. Making sure these times are accurate can go back to the BIOS time and time zone settings from the suspect computer. Investigators need access to a forensic tool that displays this information and allows sorting and analysis based on these times.

Once the actual investigation is started, it is important that all sectors be viewable. This may require restoring deleted partitions and locating hidden partitions. The sequence of steps after this can be case-specific and does not necessarily have to follow the exact order of what we will cover next, but if an investigator tends to follow a similar sequence, there is less chance of error. Obtaining hash values for all the files on the drive allows for searching and filtering based on hash values rather than file names or extensions. For example, all the Windows OS files have a consistent hash values regardless of the computer they reside on. By obtaining the hash values on the suspect drive and comparing them to the Windows hash files, all the matching files can be assumed to be identical and can be filtered out of the investigation. Similarly, if there are hash values available for files of interest, these values can be compared with the hash values on the suspect drive and everything that does not match can be filtered out. This is a common procedure in a child exploitation case.

A common next step is to conduct an Internet history search, which can involve several things including determining the sites that an individual has visited and the types of searches that have been performed using the computer. In a Windows environment, the registry can contain information on sites visited including frequency of visits and whether a site was accessed by clicking on a hyperlink or typing the URL into the browser address bar. Typing a URL can demonstrate the intent to visit a particular site, although spelling errors need to be taken into account. If a site is visited multiple times, the intent to visit is much stronger than if a site is visited one or two times.

Unallocated disk often contains the search terms that have been typed into a browser-based search engine. This can support the contention of prior knowledge or premeditation. A GREP (formally, Global Regular Expression Print) keyword search is one of the most common ways to determine the searches. Different search engines leave different artifacts, and it is important to develop search keywords that recognize this. One way to develop the keywords for the various search engines would be to conduct a few searches in the search engines and review the results that are in the address bar. This technique is described in more detail in Chapter 4.

An e-mail search is also a frequent investigative step. Some e-mail systems such as Microsoft Exchange or Lotus Notes download the e-mail messages to the individual workstation. Many Internet-based e-mail systems can be configured this way as well. This can provide a rich source of information during an investigation because full versions of the e-mail can potentially be recovered. E-mail systems such as Yahoo! and Gmail provide large disk space allocations with their free services, so many users find it attractive to just keep their e-mail in the provider's environment and not have their e-mail downloaded to their individual workstation. However, just viewing web-based e-mail in a browser frequently leaves retrievable fragments of e-mail messages in unallocated disk. I have recovered copies of 5-year-old e-mail messages from a web-based e-mail system from unallocated disk space.

Searching for keywords is another logical step in the investigation. Depending on the forensic tool being used, the keyword searches can be conducted at the same time the file hashes are being calculated, file signatures are being analyzed, and the e-mail is being searched. However, this can consume considerable resources and time, so it may be advisable to do each of these things independently. Keywords may be constructed in many ways including plain text and using GREP. Constructing keywords and executing keyword searches is a bit of an art form because if keywords are too restrictive, things may be overlooked, whereas if keywords are too loose, there may be so many search hits that it is difficult to find what the investigator is looking for. For example, if someone were searching for "botnets" and constructed the search to only look for botnets, a hit on botnet or bots would not occur. But if the search were conducted on "bot," bots, botnet, and botnets would all receive hits. However, any word that contains bot would also receive hits including words such as both and bottom. This is where constructing a GREP keyword becomes useful because a keyword can be constructed that begins with "bot" but is followed by only "net" or "s" (note the space after the "s"—spaces can play a key role in the effectiveness of keywords).

Keyword selection should take into account the type of case that is being processed. Social media sites may leave particular artifacts behind that can help reconstruct social media use. Online gaming activities have their own set of unique artifacts and related keywords. Similarly, eBay, craigslist, and Paypal may be areas where keyword searches need to be conducted. Framing the context of an investigation around certain types of use makes coming up with keywords much easier.

Particularly, in child exploitation cases, a review of graphic files on the computer is a key aspect of the investigation. Since suspects often attempt to delete evidence, all deleted graphic and video files should be recovered before conducting the search. One way this can be done is to perform a GREP search on the file header for graphic files in the unallocated space on disk. After the files are recovered, the graphic files can be viewed through the forensic tool. Alternatively, hash values can be calculated for all the graphic files on the suspect disk. These values can be compared programmatically to hash values of confirmed child exploitation graphic files. Hash values for known child exploitation files are closely held by Federal agencies and law enforcement and typically are not available for use outside of these circles. If an investigator outside of law enforcement suspects child exploitation material exists on a device they are reviewing, they should stop the investigation, not make copies, and turn over the suspected device to law enforcement.

Chat logs and artifacts from instant messaging systems can provide insight into an investigation, as can searching for game systems the computer user may be interested in. Searching for social networking sites such as Facebook and Twitter and peer-to-peer systems for sharing files are also common elements to consider in an investigation. Most computers also have log files that can provide details as to how the computer was used and maintained. If the forensic investigation is in response to a security breach such as a hacking incident, log files are one of the first things to review. Recycle bins and folders such as "Recent" that contain links to the most recently viewed files on Windows machines are other areas to commonly review, as are link files themselves. Print files and Send To files can round out the initial investigation.

After an investigation is complete, a report has to be written and the case needs to be archived. Writing a report can be very time-consuming, but this is time well spent because this is the presentation of the evidence and telling the story about what was found. Report writing is an art in and of itself and should not be glossed over. The reports that can be generated out of forensic tools usually are incomplete or lacking. Documentation as to how the investigation was conducted, who was involved, pictures and diagrams of the scene, and a general overview or abstract or summary of the report should be included. Reports can easily exceed 100 pages, so the abstract or summary becomes that much more important.

The case files, reports, and potentially copies of the forensic tools should be archived and stored in a secured environment. One reason for archiving the forensic tools that were used is that a new version of the tool may come out before the case goes to trial or otherwise comes to completion, and if a case has to be reviewed, it is important to be able to have the same tools available for the review that were used during the investigation.

Conclusion

There are many variables in determining what is appropriate and necessary in a digital forensic examination of a computer. Some cases are very targeted, so all the steps that were previously described may not be necessary. On the other hand, some cases involve even more investigation. Developing an arsenal of resources should be every investigator's goal. This arsenal would include developing a network of contacts that can assist in an investigation, whether that assistance is to help process the devices, offer suggestions, or provide psychological support. The arsenal also involves complimentary tools and techniques, education, and research capabilities. As I mentioned, the purpose of this chapter is to help an investigator understand many of the most important steps to perform in an investigation. As they say, actual mileage and conditions may vary.

References

ACPO v4.0: Good Practice Guide for Computer-Based Electronic Evidence Internet. Retrieved on July 11, 2011. http://www.7safe.com/electronic_evidence.
Internet Crime Complaint Center. (2009). Internet Crime Report. Retrieved on March 14, 2010. http://www.ic3.gov/media/annualreport/2009_IC3Report.pdf.

Other Useful Resources

Ayers, R., Jansen, W., Cilleros, N., and Daniellou, R. (2005). Cell Phone Forensic Tools: An Overview and Analysis. Retrieved on July 11, 2011. http://csrc.nist.gov/publications/nistir/nistir-7250.pdf.

Jansen, W., and Ayers, R. (2007). Guidelines on Cell Phone Forensics. National Institute of Standards and Technology. Retrieved on July 10, 2011. http://csrc.nist.gov/publications/nistpubs/800-101/SP800-101.pdf.

Lyle, J., White, D., and Ayers, R. (2008). Digital Forensics at the National Institute of Standards and Technology. Retrieved on July 11, 2011. http://www.cftt.nist.gov/NISTIR_7490.pdf.

3

DIGITAL FORENSICS TOOL KIT

Introduction

Something that can be difficult to understand is what tools to use for certain situations and how all of the information fits together to form an investigation. There are a number of variables for answering this question including the type of investigation, what the goals of the investigation are, and the fact that there is more than one way to accomplish most things in an investigation. Over time, an investigator develops an affinity for certain tools and techniques, and in time they have their "go to" tool set.

There are many challenges when describing tools in publications. There are new releases and modifications, which can make the description quickly go outdated. Similarly, tools change names, are acquired by other companies, or simply disappear from the market. For example, one useful tool—Wireshark—used to be named Ethereal. So the reader should be aware that these types of changes are inevitable, and that new developments have the potential to quickly make things go outdated in any technical field.

Computer Forensics

Computer forensics will be defined as the investigative process involving computers such as personal computers, laptops, Macintosh computers, and netbooks. Computer forensics will require one or more investigative computers. The reason for the multiple computers would be that multiple investigations may occur simultaneously, and some computers have specialized tools and functions. Use of virtualization to allow multiple virtual computers to run on one physical box may be a way to minimize hardware requirements, though RAM and things like the number of USB ports can be a limiting factor. There are vendors who configure and sell specialized forensic examination computers, which are a strong option.

Two commercial tools have dominated computer forensics for several years: Access Data's Forensic ToolKit (FTK) and Guidance Software's EnCase. Both the tools have their strengths and weaknesses, but for the most part, their capabilities are similar. Some organizations have the luxury of owning both the tools, but generally one or the other is sufficient. There are often heated discussions regarding which tool is better, and my opinion is that the companies tend to leapfrog each other with each new release. The competition translates into stronger tool options for the investigator. Both vendors have created some very good technology, and both have laid some eggs along the way as well. Version 2 of FTK was not well received in the market, and was quickly replaced with Version 3. Version 7 of EnCase was a dramatic departure in terms of interface and functionality when compared to the previous versions, which had a disorienting effect on the investigators who had experience with the previous versions. Figure 3.1 shows a screenshot of the EnCase Version 6 interface and Figure 3.2 shows a screenshot of the EnCase Version 7 interface.

There are other computer forensic options such as X-Ways, which is a European product, and open source alternatives. In addition to functionality, cost, availability of training, support, and long-term stability are the considerations for any technical purchase. The landscape can change very quickly, and it is prudent to invest in a tool

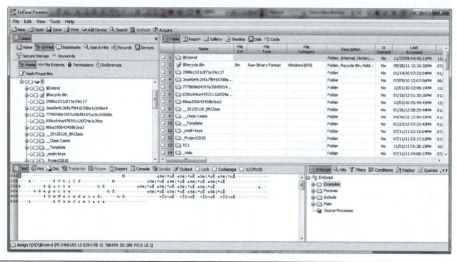

Figure 3.1 EnCase Version 6 interface.

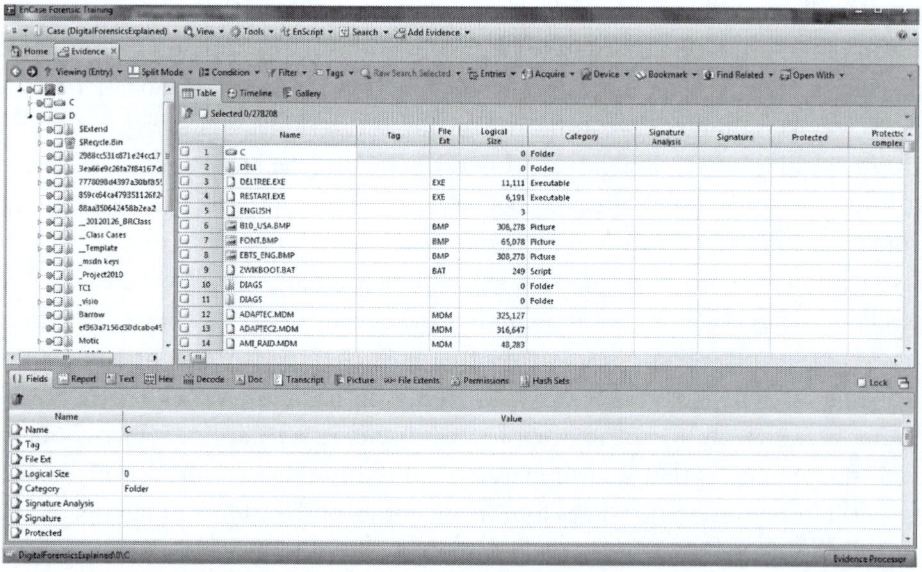

Figure 3.2 EnCase Version 7 interface.

set that has stability so that your investment can be maintained and because of the ability to find people with experience.

Computer forensic tools such as those previously mentioned can be used to image and analyze media. An advantage of an integrated tool such as EnCase or FTK is that all of the results from the various searches and operations that you perform are captured centrally, which makes the organization and reporting more straightforward. An advantage of a commercial product is that they are often tested for accuracy so that the results can be presented in a court of law. Although many open source tools have admissible findings, some have not been appropriately tested and verified, which means their findings might not be admissible in the court.

Write Blockers

Write blockers ensure that data are not altered when accessed. Booting a computer can alter hundreds of files in a computer, including access times and other file attributes. A write blocker prevents this from happening. Write blockers can be software or hardware based. Software-based write blockers use software to prevent file modification. Hardware blockers utilize a physical device to prevent file modification. Figure 3.3 shows an example of a hard drive write blocker.

An investigator will need multiple write blocker options. One hardware blocker may be needed for IDE and SATA drives, another for USB, and another for things like media cards. Some write blockers have the ability to be toggled to become a read/write interface. Why someone would have a use for write blocker that allows

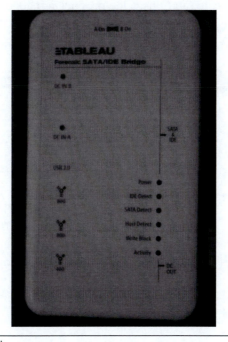

Figure 3.3 Tableau write blocker.

writing may puzzle some people, but this can be a good way to connect drives and media up to a forensic computer so that they can be wiped. Understanding how to configure the read/write capability and how to test what configuration state a blocker is in is important, so that a blocker configured with the write option is not used inadvertently in an investigation. Some vendors create blockers in different colors, and this can help distinguish write blockers from those with write capability.

Imaging

When a computer, mobile device, or other media need to be forensically analyzed, a process called imaging is often undertaken. Imaging is taking a bit for bit copy that is an exact replica of the original. A critical aspect in imaging is that it can be verified that the original version and the original are the exact duplicates. The copy can be validated to be an exact duplicate of the original by using hash algorithms such as message digest 5 (MD5) or secure hash algorithm (SHA).

In the imaging process, a computer disk drive is typically copied bit for bit to a blank drive. The drive that is used to receive the copy is wiped prior to the imaging process. Some of the ways by which this can be done include forensic tools, disk utilities, and disk imaging hardware. Once a disk is wiped, it can be verified in a similar way as wiping the drive. Forensic tools provide for a visual verification process as well. Using a disk imager is usually the fastest way to prepare a disk for imaging and to perform the imaging process. Figure 3.4 shows a picture of a Ninja disk imager.

Specialized imaging products can be used to extract data from damaged media. There are various ways these products work including the use of different types of read algorithms and hardware adaptations. One product in this class, the DeepSpar Disk Imager, modifies the way a computer communicates with a disk by preventing a read fail and end condition. Instead, the DeepSpar unit will continue attempting to recover

Figure 3.4 Ninja disk imager.

the data from the device by using alternate algorithms and techniques. In a typical computer, the read process will fail if there is a head crash. Specialized imaging tools will attempt to read all of the areas that are not impacted by the head crash rather than just producing a read failure for the entire drive.

Imaging can take a considerable amount of time. Depending on the speed of the drives, verification, and the method used, an estimate of 100 GB per hour is a rough benchmark. This may mean just imaging a 1 terabyte drive will take 10 hours. If there are multiple drives, it is easy to see how time consuming an investigation may take. Previewing a drive is a way to determine if an image is necessary. It is also possible to perform some investigative functions while the disk is being imaged.

Mobile device imaging can occupy a different place in the forensic process. Some mobile forensic products employ internal write blocking technology and simply generate a report of the contents on the device. Other mobile forensic products create an image for interrogation by the examiner. The type of process used depends on the requirements of the examination and the tools that are available.

Add-Ons and Other Technologies

Computers are often set up with a password to prevent unauthorized access to the programs and information on the device. Similarly, encryption is commonly employed as a security mechanism to protect information from unauthorized viewing. The data can technically still be accessed; they just are in an unreadable format. Algorithms are used to scramble the data, and a reverse process needs to be employed to make the data readable. Unfortunately, bad guys have adopted encryption as well. Dealing with passwords and encryption are everyday tasks for digital forensic investigators.

There are a variety of tools to work through passwords. Some let you reset Microsoft Windows passwords. Others attempt to guess the password using attack methods such as dictionary and brute force. Encryption tools such as TrueCrypt lock a container, partition, or drive with a password. When the password is entered, the contents are accessible in unencrypted format. Dictionary attacks use words or combinations of words as a way to guess a password. Dictionaries used in the attacks can include common dictionaries in a variety of languages. There can also be specialized dictionaries of acronyms or slang. A brute force attack generates combinations of letters, numbers, and special characters in an attempt to guess the password. Some tools allow the investigator to seed the password tool with known aspects of the password, to shorten the password cracking process.

An additional decryption and password guessing mechanism is the use of rainbow tables. Passwords are often stored in a hashed format rather than plain text. A decryption tool would need to hash the words in dictionary and then use the hashes in the password attack. Rainbow tables streamline this process by hashing a dictionary. Efficiency is gained, as the decryption tool does not need to hash the dictionary during the attack.

The more complex a password is, the longer it can take to guess it. Depending on the technologies used, eight-character passwords that have numbers, letters, and special characters can take months or years to crack. Specialized decryption computers can be utilized to speed up the attack. A graphics card's GPU can be orders of magnitude faster for decryption than using a computer's RAM. Gaming computers can be configured with multiple parallel high-speed graphics cards with dramatic increases in decryption capabilities.

Audio, video, and graphic files are common evidence that must be processed by an investigator. The files often need enhancement, so familiarity with tools that can provide this capability is a key skill. Situations where this comes into play include working through surveillance video, processing pictures with poor resolution or focus, and counterfeit cases. Software such as Photoshop is a common choice for this purpose, and there are many specialized technologies that provide even more capability.

Computer forensic tools have built in file viewers, but there are times when other viewers are needed. Some of the commonly used viewers are Irfanview, offline HTML viewers such as NavRoad, VideoLAN's VLC media player, and Microsoft Office. Compressed files are also frequently encountered, so a tool such as WinRAR comes in handy for access. Although a hex editor is a common feature of computer forensic tools, sometimes an external hex editor comes in handy. Similarly, a hash calculator such as HashCalc is useful for generating file hashes.

Calculating file offsets and base conversions is useful in working through file systems to find file fragments and artifacts. Assigning a shortcut to a calculator on the task bar of the forensic computer is a way to gain handy access. A base converter such as FeelTheBase translates decimal, binary, hex, and IP, and is another add-on for the examiner's tool kit.

For examinations that involve malware, a process monitor such as Sysinternal's Process Explorer will display process in more detail than the Window's Task Monitor. Figure 3.5 shows an example of the information available in Process Explorer.

Tools such as Wireshark, NetStat, and TCPView will provide network and communication information that an investigator can use in determining malware configuration and capability. Particularly when a machine is live, port status and communication addresses can be useful in tracing malware activity and also when responding to hacking incidents.

Speaking of live machines, a way to image and process RAM can be another way to work through a malware or hacking forensic case, as well as to locate passwords. A USB drive containing a small utility that dumps the contents of RAM to the USB drive is a typical way to capture the information. A RAM dump is not formatted, so a tool that can process the dump to find the information of interest is another piece that needs to be part of an examiner's tool kit. HBGary is a tool that can provide this type of analysis. HBGary was a key tool used to track down the parties responsible in a significant hack of Google, Morgan Stanley, and many other organizations.

It would be remise on my part to not mention the role of antivirus (AV) software in the digital forensic process. Malware investigation can provide insight in determining the validity of an alibi, as well as in determining the penetration of malware within an organization. It is not unusual for someone to claim a malware defense when accused of a computer crime. The stance is based on the premise that they did

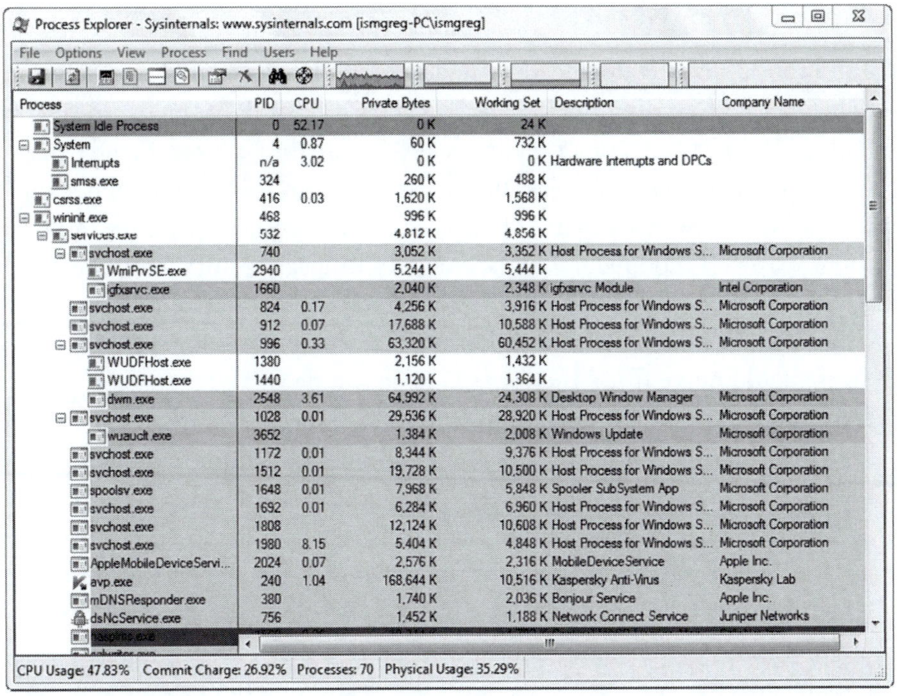

Figure 3.5 Process Explorer.

not do anything wrong—rather—their computer was infected with malware and the controller of the malware was responsible for the criminal activity. AV software can be used to help determine whether there is malware on the suspect's computer. If there is, it is incumbent on the investigator to determine whether the malware has the capability that is claimed. Taken further, the malware may have the capability, but the question is whether it has been configured to perform the tasks that are claimed in the defense.

A response team in a hacking situation must quickly determine what is being hacked, how, when, what has been breached, and the resulting impact. Malware often plays a role in this type of situation, and is an area of growing concern for digital forensic investigators. Both of these topics—the malware alibi and malware penetration—open up the area of malware forensics, which is beyond the scope of this book.

These are just some of the many add-ons and other capabilities that are possible additions to a forensic examiner's tool kit that can transcend its capabilities from basic to complex situations. This list is by no means exhaustive, and there are many other useful tools that justify being mentioned but have not been. There are many books and other resources available, which provide more information on these and other tools. The purpose of this chapter was simply to bring an awareness of some of the tools and how they fit into the investigative process, not to be a tutorial on how to use each one.

Tools

A digital forensic investigator needs a wide range of tools including screw drivers, sockets, hex keys, grounding device, suction cups, a flash light, tape, zip ties, string, scissors, pliers, wire cutters, razor blades, labels, a camera, blanket, Faraday bag, storage bags/cases, magnifying glass, extension cord, various cables and connectors, pencil, paper/log book, permanent marker, air sickness bags, latex gloves, and a black light. Screw drivers should include standard and Philips, hex, torx, star, and tri. Game systems such as the Wii use tri screws. Understand that magnetized screw drivers can impact the data on a hard drive and harm other computer components. The screw driver sizes should range from micro/eye glass to standard.

Suction cups are useful to help remove and replace monitor components when pulling a drive from an iMac. A flash light is used in low-light conditions such as working under desks and in closets. A backpacker's headlight works well because it is a hands-free solution. It is nice to have a clean blanket to use as a barrier on a dirty floor or other surface. Sometimes an investigator finds that they have to lay on a floor and it is much more pleasant to be able to lay on a blanket. Blankets also come in handy to use for pads when transporting computers and other devices.

Extension cords can serve multiple purposes. A short cord on a power strip may be all that is needed in one instance, but in another, it may be necessary to have a long extension cord that can reach a circuit in another room or other location, perhaps due to a bad circuit or as a way to avoid the circuit in the room the investigation is occurring. In other words, having a 100-ft. extension cord is not a bad idea.

A pencil and paper is useful for notes, but it is also useful for mapping a room or location where a computer and peripheral equipment are located. This can be helpful in refreshing the examiner's mind prior to testifying, as well as helping to document the scene. Color pencils can help provide color-coded details.

A hard drive needs to be handled carefully when it is pulled from a computer. Sometimes the drive is pulled and the computer is left at the site. Antistatic bags are made specifically for this purpose, and the bag that a new hard drive comes in can be used to store subsequent drives—so do not throw them away. I have found that air sickness bags can also work in a pinch. Their original purpose can also come in handy when an investigator has to sort through the trash some cases present.

A forensic examiner told me a story about how he sent a uniformed officer out to seize a computer. The officer had a brand new squad car, and he drove out to the site, seized the computer, and secured it in the front seat of his squad car with the seat belt. When he carried the computer into the lab, the examiner asked the officer whether he lighted the computer. The officer did not understand what the examiner meant and set the computer down on a table. The examiner took out a black light and held it near the computer. The examiner told the officer that the case was a sex crime and the black light lit the computer up with proteins. Needless to say, the officer changed uniforms and took his car in for upholstery cleaning. He also learned what the latex gloves were for.

Mobile Forensics Tools

For the purpose of this discussion, mobile forensics will include cell phones, tablets, GPS devices, and MP3 players such as iPods. Just like computer forensics, there are many open-source and vendor products in this category. Guidance Software and Access Data have integrated mobile support into their computer forensic products, but the level of device support tends to lag some of the leading mobile forensic vendors. Commercial products that support a wide range of devices include offerings from Cellebrite, Paraben, Micro Systemation, and Oxygen. Some vendors such as Katana focus on a specific niche such as Apple's iOS and attempt to be the best in that market.

An interesting variable with mobile forensics is that there can be a regional implication. For example, some vendors tweak device design and/or configuration based on where the device will be deployed. I have met with an engineer from Micro Systemation who typically buys phones and devices when he visits a different region of the United States or another country, because there can be intricate differences in seemingly the same device depending on where it is purchased and deployed. New phones and enhancements are released at least every few days, and this creates a support challenge for mobile forensic product engineers. The wide assortment of interface cables is yet another challenge in maintaining a mobile forensic tool kit.

Even more so than computer forensics, having more than one mobile forensic option is very valuable because the level of support for each device can vary considerably. Logical extraction, physical extraction, and file system extraction can provide dramatically different results, particularly as it relates to recovering deleted artifacts. Generally, products that provide both logical and physical extraction support more devices at the logical level than they do at the physical level. Often, a physical extraction will provide the majority of what a logical extraction provides plus more detail. Therefore, physical extraction capabilities are potentially the most valuable of the two. File system extraction can be particularly useful in recovering deleted artifacts. Software write blocking is frequently employed in mobile forensics.

There are several considerations when determining the most appropriate mobile forensic solution. Factors such as price, support, ease of use, stability of vendor, stability of product, and level of extract capability are key issues. Mobile forensic products tend to cost more than computer forensic products—and in some cases, considerably more. The annual maintenance for some mobile forensic products can be a few thousand dollars per license. Product support includes frequency of updates, number of new features and device support that tend to be with each update, and timely response and resolution to support questions are important factors.

Ease of use varies considerably within the mobile forensic market. Some tools operate much like a computer forensic tool whereas others operate as a stand-alone device. Cellebrite uses a stand-alone device that connects to the device of interest and pushes the information to a USB drive or external device such as a computer. There are a few

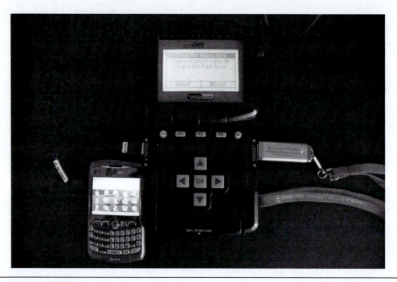

Figure 3.6   Cellebrite UFED.

keys to navigate an onboard menu, and it can be operated by someone with very little training. However, searching through the physical and file system extracts to find file fragments is similar to using other products. Figure 3.6 shows a Cellebrite Universal Forensic Extraction Device (UFED).

Stability of vendor and stability of product can be two different things. Some companies may be stable, but their products may have bugs and other problems. It is important to look closely at this because there are vendors and products in this market space that consistently perform poorly. Length of time in the market is not necessarily a key indicator of the vendor or the product, because some of the newer vendors have some interesting products and some of the older vendors have some of the less stable offerings.

Extraction capability is perhaps the most important variable when using mobile forensic products. Two products that claim to support a particular device at the physical level may produce different results, as one product may extract far more information than the other. One product may extract 500 text messages from a device, whereas another product may extract 1000. It is very common in a mobile forensics investigation to use multiple products to get the most complete forensic perspective as possible.

Visual Analysis

Finding artifacts and information is only a part of the challenge facing an investigator. Analyzing and interpreting the information can be a difficult task. Temporal analysis involves looking at the time events occur to help interpret findings. There are timeline tools available in many forensic tools, but visual analysis tools can be used to sort through information and find patterns and other characteristics to help put together the puzzle that is digital forensics. Visual analysis tools are discussed in more detail in the mobile forensics chapter.

Secured Storage

An examiner needs a safe and secure way to transport devices back to the lab. Blankets and seat belts are the poor man's way to transport, whereas padded Pelican® cases are the preferred method. This has the added advantage of being weatherproof and providing some degree of shock protection should something be dropped.

Once in the lab, the devices need a secure place to be stored. This may be a secured room, a safe, storage locker, or some combination. How storage is handled is one of the most important aspects of a case, because the chain of custody can be a weak point that can cause a case to be lost. Personally, I like the option of having a safe that is mounted into the wall or floor. A gun case can work well for this. Physical security can include locked doors, key card access, video surveillance, and redundant security methods.

Secured storage of tools is an area that is often overlooked. In addition to wear and tear, concerns can include artifacts from an investigation being cached or stored on the investigative devices. Wiping and rebuilding computers and tools used on cases prevents the problem of evidence leeching out, but wiping and rebuilding is usually done after a case is completed—if it is done at all. However, this does not address the fact that many investigations run on for weeks, so it is impractical to wipe and rebuild in a way that would work in that environment. That is why secured storage of tools is necessary.

Damaged Media

Retrieving information from damaged media is a specialized application of digital forensics. Storage media can be damaged by normal daily use or by intentional mishandling. There are organizations that provide recovery services that retrieve information from damaged devices. A well-known example of this was the recovery of information from a disk drive from the Columbia Space Shuttle disaster. I have received research funding through a grant from the National Science Foundation investigating how damage impacts the data resident on storage media. Through this research, I have found that the type of data that is stored on the media may impact the degree to which it is recoverable, particularly with optical media such as a DVD. The way that I was able to determine this was using a digital laser microscope, which is a highly specialized piece of equipment.

Summary

The application of digital forensics is a broad and evolving field that necessitates a broad and evolving tool kit. There are a variety of options available to an investigator for computer, mobile, and malware forensics that provide insight into what a device has been used for and how the actions can be explained. Developing and maintaining strong skills in digital forensics is an arduous task and can consume a lot of time and energy. Particularly when it comes to malware investigation, digital forensic investigators find themselves up against a difficult environment and prodigious challenge. Proficiency in using a variety of tools positions an investigator to be able to best meet the challenges inherent in the cyber world.

4

INTERNET AND E-MAIL EXAMINATIONS

Introduction

E-mail is an interesting phenomenon in that it often documents a person's activities and choices in a written format—signed, dated, and with witnesses (recipients) no less. E-mail can help prove that something happened, provide an alibi, or provide a noose that hangs someone. E-mail is one of the most important areas that an examiner concentrates on during an examination.

Internet activity provides a window into an individual's interests and inclinations, and reviewing the artifacts left behind by his or her activity can lend significant insight into what an individual has been doing. There are a lot of potential places to look for clues of Internet behavior including chat and messaging logs, peer to peer (P2P) actions, search engine searches, Internet history, social networking activity, and virus and malware footprints. It is worth noting that the precise detail of how to investigate each of these areas changes over time, so understanding how to adapt to these changes is a skill that distinguishes the average investigators from those who are exceptional.

E-Mail

People commonly have multiple e-mail addresses, and they are often used for specific purposes. One e-mail address may be for work, another for general social activity, and yet another may be used in coordination with things like gaming or other recreational pursuits. E-mail addresses are often usernames on websites, so once e-mail addresses are uncovered, performing keyword searches on the portion prior to the @ sign may be a way to discover Internet sites and other activities that were previously missed.

One of the first e-mail searches that I perform is to create keywords for as many free e-mail accounts as I can think of: @yahoo.com, @hotmail.com, @gmail.com, and so on. This will often create a large search result set, but the potential payoff for finding the information is substantial. After I find all of the e-mail addresses, I often create a set of keywords for full e-mail address—such as badguy@yahoo.com or just badguy—because the first search may create too much volume to effectively find the information that is of interest.

Another thing that I find useful is to perform searches on names of cities, landmarks, hotels, and highways in an area, as these often lead to e-mail or messages of interest. Think about unique words that might be in an e-mail, and use a search based on that to find e-mail addresses. I have used this "work backward" technique to help solve civil cases, as messages fragments may be in unallocated without an e-mail address header.

E-mail headers can be used to track where the messages originated and where they routed from. Sometimes the header is stripped out or unreadable, but if it is intact, the physical address can be found. The American Registry of Internet Numbers (www.arin.net) can be used to track down the registered contact and possible physical address from where an e-mail message originated.

Chat and Messaging Logs

There are countless ways that people can utilize chat and messaging to communicate. Instant Messenger, Yahoo! Messenger, video chat, social networking sites, and texting are just a few of the ways that are commonly utilized. It is not uncommon for people to use multiple methods, change from a previous method to a new method, or utilize multiple accounts for the same method. Keeping this in mind can help prevent overlooking evidence.

One of the ways to determine whether a person is actively using chat and messaging is to look at what programs autostart when a person logs into his or her computer. For Windows machines, this would include looking in the Software hive of the registry. There can be more than one place to look, but a useful location is the ShellServiceObjectDelayLoad. Once explorer.exe has loaded, it will execute the values in this subkey.

Another way to determine whether a person has been using chat and messaging is to look at the installed programs. In the event that you suspect someone has deleted their chat and messaging tools, you can look in the registry for artifacts left behind from the uninstall process. There may also be some support files that are still on the computer. Working with the message boards to network with other investigators is a good way to find information specific to a tool or technology, and this may be an effective way to receive feedback and ideas on how to work through challenges.

Similar to e-mail, it is possible to find chat activity in unallocated through GREP searches and reviews of logs. If the investigation centers on finding information related to a particular type of behavior, then performing keyword searches on words and phrases that are representatives of that behavior may uncover fragments of interest. Remember to consider locations, actions, and slang when building keywords for searches.

Peer-to-Peer

P2P networking sites are used for file sharing, though the practice is not always legitimate. There are many sites that fall into this category, with new sites emerging frequently. The BitTorrent protocol is used to share files that are often broken up into pieces for later reassembly. Because partial files are shared rather than full files, it is more difficult to shut the site down for piracy or other actions. The sites involved with this activity can come up and go down quickly, which makes it even harder for law enforcement to pursue them. From a digital forensics perspective, performing some research to find out what the current popular BitTorrent sites are and what types of files, programs, and artifacts might need to be installed to use them is necessary, because this is one of the fastest changing areas in the digital forensics.

It is not unusual for someone to have a computer that is dedicated to P2P activity. Finding an unusually large music collection on a computer that does not have P2P loaded may be a tip-off that there is another computer floating around out there that has not been seized. The other aspect of this is that people involved in P2P often have multiple hard drives. P2P cases often evolve around copyright infringement such as music—or illegal activity such as child exploitation. Unfortunately, examiners usually spend their time dealing with the latter.

Search Engine Activity

Perhaps the most efficient way to develop keyword to determine search engine activity is to bring up a few search engines and conduct searches. A pattern will emerge that can be useful in keyword definition. Similar to other areas in the technology, the search engine patterns do change. Creating a keyword based on how Google presents a search term today is not necessarily the same as it was a year or two ago. The implication is that an examiner will need to create what I will call generations of search engine patterns. The examiners often review computers that are a few years old, so the keywords need to reflect this, otherwise information may be missed.

Each of the following figures provide ideas on how to build keywords to use in keyword searches in forensic tools for search engines based on the sample search criteria "digital forensics."

For the Bing search engine:

www.**bing.com**/search?q=digital+forensics&qs=n&form=QBLH&pc

The keyword for this type of Bing search would be "bing.com/search?q="
For the Dogpile search engine:

www.**dogpile.com**/search/web?fcoid=417&fcop=topnav&fpid=27&q=digital+forensics&ql=

The keyword for this type of Dogpile search would be "dogpile.com/search/web?"
For the Google search engine:

www.**google.com**/#hl=en&output=search&sclient=psy-ab&q=digital+forensics&oq:

The keyword for this type of Google search would be "google.com/#hl=en"

An important point when developing search engine keywords is to test several search criteria and look closely for the pattern in the URL bar on the browser. Particularly with Google, there is often significant variation. The investigator should also realize that this will bring up all searches that meet the criteria—so the results could be thousands of records.

Internet History

Where an examiner looks for Internet History depends on the browsers that were used on the suspect computer. Internet Explorer leaves artifacts in index.dat files, and the examiner has to remember that there are multiple index.dat files on a Windows computer, and they are used for different purposes. Information that is captured includes the URL of the last several websites visited, the last time it was visited, and how many times it was visited. Files that were opened with Internet Explorer can also be logged in the index.dat file. Although it is also often possible to determine whether a web address was typed or accessed via hyperlink, it is important to remember that Internet History is limited. There may also be information in Temp folders related to websites visited. Other browsers such as Firefox and Chrome also leave artifacts on a computer that can provide similar insight, and some of these artifacts may be in browser databases.

Cookies are another way to determine what websites have been visited, as websites commonly place one or more cookies on a website. Cookies may also provide usernames for websites that are used by the person operating the computer.

For both Internet History and E-mail discovery, it is useful to rebuild the web pages when possible. This can be accomplished by carving out the html file and opening it in an external viewer to render the web page. This may make a more compelling exhibit in a report than a text bookmark. An offline tool such as NavRoad will likely work better for rendering a web page than a browser.

Other things that can provide clues to Internet History are browser add-ons such as toolbars, extensions, players, and applications. There are add-on tools that assist in activities such as file sharing, pirating video and intellectual property, and customization. In addition, bookmarks, favorites, shortcuts, stored passwords, and browser settings can also provide support for user activities.

Something that needs to be pointed out is that as website addresses are discovered, many of them may not be recognized by the examiner. That may mean that the examiner needs to go to the websites to see what their purposes are. Be very careful as the websites may drop malware, which may infect the examiner's computer. The sites may also be where illegal activity takes place. My suggestion is that a separate research computer or virtual machine be used for researching these sites to reduce the risk of infection—and so that fragments of the website can be easily wiped out with a rebuild/restore of the research computer. Related to this, websites store IP addresses and you might not want them to get your IP address. Consider the use of an anonymizer to protect your identity.

Social Networking and Gaming

Social networking sites such as Facebook, Twitter, and LinkedIn are among the most common sites visited on the web, and should be part of all Internet investigations. As in other areas, it is common for a person to have more than one account; so an examiner should take the time to try and identify all potential accounts that a person may be using. Account names often have some sort of correlation to e-mail accounts, so finding one account name can lead to two interest trails such as social networking and e-mail to follow. If you find account names, Google can be your friend—performing Google searches on the account names may lead to considerable information. One of the advantages of social networking sites is that they can be rich in providing background information on an individual, as well as other potential subjects of interest. Chapter 9 is devoted to Social Media Forensics, which provides additional information not included in this section.

If an examiner is unsure of where to start with regard to discovering social networking information, an option is to simply create keyword searches on "facebook" and other popular or relevant sites, review the results, and refine the searches. Smartphones may have significant information regarding social networking activities, and may be another area to look for clues to assist with building keywords.

In many ways, gaming is another form of social networking. Popular gaming sites and theme sites that are consistent with what the investigator is looking for are also potential interest trails to follow. This could also include virtual worlds and similar destinations. The type of computer that is seized can be a tip-off in indicating whether the owner is a gaming enthusiast, as gaming computers tend to be higher end machines with improved graphics and peripheral devices. It is also possible that much of the online gaming that a person conducts is done through a game system such as an Xbox, Wii, or Play Station.

Malware and Viruses

The presence of malware and viruses can serve multiple purposes for an investigator. It is possible that the investigation is attempting to determine whether the computer owner is a malware author or manager. Another situation is to determine the source of infections. Yet another situation is that the computer owner may claim a malware defense—something along the lines of "I didn't do it! There must have been a virus on my computer."

There has to be development tools somewhere if someone is an author of malware. This may or may not be on the computer that the investigator has seized—or it may be in a protected volume or virtual machine contained within the computer. Another potential piece of information would be to perform keyword searches on malware websites, bulletin boards, and Internet Relay Chat (IRC) artifacts. Again, look for possible usernames. If usernames are found, remember your Google friend and perform Google searches on the usernames.

Determining the source of an infection can be a temporal study checking the directory entries on files such as modified, accessed, and created times (often called MAC times). When looking at a network of computers, the goal is to find the earliest MAC times within the group to locate the potential initial infection location. This can be a time-consuming and arduous process. Some ways to shorten the investigation time would be to look for possible e-mail infection sources, shared media, and start with those that tend to be somewhat loose in the computer practices.

Investigating the virus defense is not as difficult as it would seem. First of all, the person claiming a virus defense would have to have a virus on his or her computer. Secondly, the virus needs to be active and capable of performing the activity that the person claims. A tool like NetStat can be useful in determining whether this is the case. If the virus does not exist on the computer, and it is not active and capable of performing the activity the person claims, the person is in for a world of hurt. On the contrary, if both of these things turn out to be true, the only thing left to check is whether the person self-infected himself or herself to create an alibi. If the investigator cannot prove self-infection, then it would be very difficult to convince a jury that the virus defense is a ploy cooked up by the suspect.

Trojans and key loggers can have a lot of similarities in terms of what the malware does and what an investigator looks for. For one thing, trojan, key logger, and keylogger are good keywords to search on. On a Windows machine, some of the areas to look for artifacts are similar, including the Registry. An investigator should look for startup programs and Registry-specified executable behavior (executables are often called "e- × -e's"). A person may attempt to remove malware, but later he or she finds that it reappears. Malware can be configured so that it reinstalls every time and executable is run. So a scenario might be to remove the malware and then run a program such as Microsoft Word—which is an executable and would reinstall the malware.

Determining how malware impacts a machine in terms of files that are modified, settings that are changed, and new files that are created can take considerable effort. One way to do this is the virgin method. The virgin method is to build a fresh machine with a clean install, create a hash set of the files on the computer (the virgin hash set), infect the computer with the malware, hash all of the files on the computer, and then filter out the files that are in the virgin hash set. The remaining files will be those that were modified or created.

Every file or collection of files can be run through an algorithm to obtain a hash value. Algorithms such as Message Digest 5 (MD5) and Secure Hash Algorithm 1 (SHA-1) are commonly used for this purpose, and their accuracy is very high. The MD5 algorithm is 128 bit, whereas the SHA-1 algorithm is 160 bit. The translation in terms of probability of two different files generating the same MD5 hash is something like the number of millimeters from the earth to the sun and back, which is highly unlikely. The probability of two files generating the same SHA-1 hash is even more unlikely. Although it would be an extreme condition where two files generate the same MD5 or SHA-1 hash, research has shown that it is possible. This situation is known as a hash collision. However, to my knowledge, there is no documented instance of the MD5 and SHA-1 hash values of a single file both having a successful collision. In other words, computing an MD5 and SHA-1 hash for the file hashtest.txt. Though extremely rare, it may be possible to create a file that generates the same MD5 or SHA-1 hash, but it is not possible to create a file that is different from hashtest.txt that generates the same MD5 and SHA-1 hash value. For this reason, a lot of forensic tools now generate hash values for a file in both the MD5 and SHA-1 formats.

Perhaps a less confusing way to look at this would be to consider a person's first and last name, along with date of birth, as an MD5 hash. It is unlikely to have a duplicate, but it is possible. Then think of someone's first and last name, along with names of parents, as a SHA-1 hash. It is unlikely to have a duplicate, but it is possible. The example that comes to mind is former boxer George Foreman. He has several sons who are all named George Foreman. His sons would be an example of a SHA-1 hash collision. However, their dates of birth (part of our MD5 has example) are different, so the combination of the MD5 and SHA-1 hashes for each person maintains uniqueness. Now keep in mind that the MD5 and SHA-1 algorithms are far more accurate than what was used in our example, where things were simplified for illustration purposes.

Getting back to creating hash sets and our virgin method of determining impact from malware. Forensic tools such as Guidance Software's EnCase and Access Data's FTK can be used to calculate the hash values for all of the files on a computer. The hash values for all of these files can be tagged as related, which are known as a hash set. We could then infect our computer with malware, which would modify some of the files on the computer and introduce new files. At this point, we can compute hash values for all of the files on the computer to create another hash set. We could then compare each hash set and filter out all files that have the same hash value. The only files remaining would be those that were changed by the malware, as well as the new files that were introduced by the malware. This makes our investigation much more focused. There are many other tools that can be used to compute hash values for files that examiners find useful. I find HashCalc to be beneficial because it calculates several hash values simultaneously. Figure 4.1 depicts calculating hash values of a file using HashCalc.

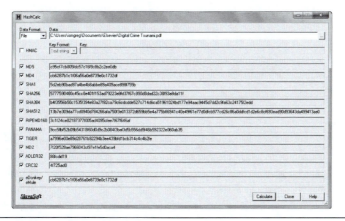

Figure 4.1   Calculating hash values using HashCalc.

Hash values have many purposes in digital forensic investigations and are commonly used to conclusively identify child pornography. Several law enforcement and government agencies maintain hash sets of known child pornography images that examiners can use similar to our malware hash set filtering example.

There are a number of ways to obtain malware for research purposes. Websites such as www.malwaredomainlist.com and http://contagiodump.blogspot.com are sources of viruses and other information. There are known websites that are well-known locations as malware havens, and SPAM is a frequent source as well. Developing a library of malware is a good way to research the broader impacts. Imaging an infected machine or disk is a good way to capture the environment for study.

Summary

Inevitably, new tools will emerge and new tools and techniques will need to be developed to forensically mine the information needed in an investigation. The virgin method is not necessarily the most efficient way to determine the impact of actions on a computer, but it is effective and can serve well if all other avenues fail. Remember your friend Google, participate in the forums, and network with other investigators. Digital forensics is a force against the dark side, but the dark side is formidable and we as investigators need to work smart and help each other.

5

Mobile Forensics

Introduction

Mobile devices include cell phones, smartphones, and table devices. Cell phones and smartphones share many common capabilities, but smartphones can also perform many tasks often associated with a computer. Many mobile devices include one or more cameras, a geographic positioning system (GPS), and other technologies that are often linked to the Internet. A cell phone is actually a specialized radio with an antenna, microphone, speaker, keypad, display, and battery. Mobile phones operate via frequencies over wireless cell networks. These cell networks are maintained by towers and switching stations.

Mobile Phone Technology

There are several cell phone technologies including Global System for Mobile Communications (GSM), Code Division Multiple Access (CDMA), Time Division Multiple Access (TDMA), and Integrated Digital Enhanced Network (iDEN) (Jansen and Ayers, 2007). GSM is the most common international standard and CDMA has a large presence in the United States. A great deal of time could be spent detailing these technologies, so this will be limited to a brief overview of primarily GSM and CDMA. These two competing technologies tend to leapfrog each other in terms of speed and features, which combined with other factors makes it difficult to say one is absolutely better than the other. GSM phones use a Subscriber Identity Module, commonly known as a SIM card. A SIM card ties the phone to the network and can be swapped between devices. The SIM card is of interest to a forensic examiner because it often contains considerable information such as an address book and configuration data. SIM cards are often made of a paper or plastic material stamped with electronic features, so care must be taken when handling them. The SIM card contains the International Mobile Subscriber Identifier (IMSI), which identifies the subscriber to the network.

There are a lot of variables in both GSM and CDMA technologies, such as cell size and frequency. One distinction is that adjacent cells in a CDMA network can use the same frequency, so this allows for a soft handover of a signal between cells as the call can have multiple connections. When a call is being transferred between cells, the stronger connection is established and then the weaker connection is dropped. In contrast, GSM relies on a hard handover, which means that a call uses only one channel. When a call is being transferred between cells, the connection is momentarily dropped before the new connection is maintained. Many devices that utilize a hard handover can reestablish the previous connection if the new connection cannot be completed, assuming the previous connection is still available.

Subscriber identifying information is included in the International Mobile Equipment Identity (IMEI) for GSM phones and the Electronic Serial Number (ESN) for Verizon phones. The IMEI, which identifies a device to the network, may also be known as the Mobile Equipment Identifier (MEID) on a CDMA network as the MEID was created to replace the ESN. These numbers or codes are often displayed on a sticker on a device. Many equipment manufacturers prefer to place the sticker near or under the battery.

How a Call Is Made

Cellular telephones operate on a short-wave wireless connection from a transmitter. When a cell phone is turned on, it searches for a signal from a cell phone tower to make a connection. When the connection is made, the phone transmits the identifying information to the network to give the network awareness of the phone. The network verifies the identifying information and services are established. There are several variables that determine how a call is made. For example, a call from a cell phone to a land phone needs to be switched between the cell network and the landline network in order to complete the call. A call from a cell phone to another cell phone may stay within the cell network, but it may be switched from the cell network to a landline network and then back to the cell network. One example of this might be a cell phone in the United States making a call to a cell phone in Europe. Other reasons for switching between a cell network and a landline network may include the physical distance being too far for a cell technology to communicate, service, geographical, economical, political, or even contractual reasons. If a person is moving when placing the call, the call is transferred between cell towers for call management.

Most cell phones and mobile devices are digital, which means that they communicate through binary code. The communication is through the ultra high frequency (UHF) radio spectrum. Within this spectrum, there is a frequency range designated for cell phone communication. This frequency range can vary among countries or continents. Most GSM phones operate on a wider range of frequency bands than CDMA.

Forensic Challenges

Mobile devices present a unique set of forensic challenges compared to computers. One of the most evident differences is the number of states that a mobile device can be found in. Owen and Thomas (2011) describe the five states of mobile devices as follows:

- Off—Powered off and the battery is removed.
- Nascent state—No user data (factory fresh).

- Quiescent state—The device appears to be inactive even though it is actually performing functions.
- Semiactive state—The device is waiting for a set time to perform a function.
- Active state—The device is powered on and tasks are being performed on it.

Adding to the complexity of mobile devices are factors such as a wide variety of devices, operating systems, and feature combinations of the various device states. There are many different menu systems, keyboard types, and input methods, as well as security mechanisms. A forensic examiner needs to be familiar with these systems, methods, and mechanisms in order to be able to effectively process these devices. Online vendor websites and video sites such as YouTube can be useful in building understanding with the devices that the examiner is not familiar with.

An ongoing debate in computer forensics has been how a computer is seized. Whether or not the power should be pulled from the back of the computer or whether the machine should be shut down normally has been discussed at length. The proponents of disconnecting the power argued that the machine was in a state more representative of what it was when it was seized, and that routines that may be triggered to destroy the information on the computer would potentially be circumvented. The proponents of bringing the machine down normally argued that the disruption in power may corrupt files on the computer. What was lost in the discussion until more recently was that considerable information useful to the investigation may exist in RAM, and once the power is terminated, the contents in RAM would likely be gone. In addition to the information about running processes, RAM may also contain passwords, server names, and IP addresses.

There are similar challenges when seizing mobile devices with regard to power state. If a device is powered down, a password or passcode may be needed to access its contents when it is powered back on. Many mobile devices have features that wipe or reset to factor settings if an incorrect password or passcode is entered a preset number of times. If a device remains in an active state, it can be potentially wiped remotely. One way of preventing remote access or wiping is to place the device in a Faraday container. This prevents communication with the device. Attaching a self-contained power supply to the device may be necessary to maintain battery life as the loss of communication means that the device will continually search for service, which can quickly reduce battery life. Simply connecting a power supply from an electrical outlet or vehicle electrical adapter to the device and then placing the device into the Faraday container is not sufficient as the electrical cord can act like an antenna and defeat the Faraday properties of the container.

An important consideration with mobile devices is the speed and methods devices can be reset, thereby deleting data. This can include algorithms based on passcodes when accessing the device, remote wiping, and time-sensitive information. Some mobile devices keep track of cell tower information that a person may be using when they are making a call—and in some cases just when driving by a tower when they are not making a call. This was a strong issue in the news in 2011 and surfaced the issue of consumer privacy (Paul, 2011). Changes were made, but there can still be devices that contain this information. However, it is in a state that is more difficult to access forensically and the data are stored for a shorter time frame than it was previously. The implications for the forensic analysts are that they have to be aware of ways that data may be deleted, and they also have to be cognoscente of time-sensitive algorithms that may delete data based on date/time information.

One of the more frustrating aspects of mobile forensics is that forensic tool support of devices can be spotty. For example, a forensic tool may advertise that it supports a few thousand types of devices, but the level of support is often different. For example, the forensic tool may extract text messages, address book, and many other artifacts from a device from one manufacturer, but the tool may only extract address book from a different device. Often there is a misperception that devices have similar support and that similar artifacts can be extracted from all supported devices. That just is not the case, and it is one reason why it makes sense to equip a mobile forensic lab with multiple forensic tools.

Forensic Process

Handheld devices are considered embedded systems, which are systems that primarily do one thing. Functionality has been expanded in mobile devices such as tablets and similar devices, so there is an overlap in capabilities between handhelds and mobile devices. Because of this, the following discussion will treat handheld and mobile devices as synonymous even though there may be some distinguishing characteristics between the two. Characteristics that complicate forensics include the active device nature of handhelds and mobile devices, as well as the push technology often used in this platform. Storage capacities have historically been relatively small, but with advances in cloud technology, local storage is not a limiting factor in terms of device functionality. Mobile device forensics is done in part by active imaging, so all of these characteristics need to be taken into consideration.

Mobile forensics can become an exercise in adaptability because of the vast number of devices and the rapid rate of innovation. Tools such as Cellebrite and XRY support thousands of devices, but a significant number of devices are not supported, and many of those that are do not enjoy full support. For example, a forensic tool may be able to extract the address book entries, but not text messages. It would seem that having access to tools such as Cellebrite and XRY would put an investigator in a good position to conduct an investigation, and in many situations that is the case. However, I have encountered a number of times where I have tried to image and analyze a device only to come up with little or no information. It is important to have multiple tools that have overlapping capabilities. It is not unusual to acquire a supported device with one tool and get different results than the acquisition from a second tool. The important distinction is to realize that one tool may do a better job with text message, whereas another tool may do a better job with e-mail. The results do not contradict each other—they supplement each other. For example, tool A might recover 50 text messages and tool B might recover 60. Between the two tools, there might be the same 50 text messages, with tool B recovering 10 additional. Another example might be that tool A does not recover deleted images, whereas tool B does. This is similar to having a fresh set of eyes review something that you are stuck on.

It is important to practice diligence when evaluating forensic tools for use, particularly in the mobile forensics market. Some tool providers oversell the capabilities and stability of their products. My purpose is not to recommend or blacklist tools, but I would strongly suggest conducting thorough hands-on evaluations and performing reference checks to ensure whether tools operate as advertised. There are tools in this market space that are among the most frustrating experiences in terms of performance, stability, and vendor support of any aspect of digital forensics.

Following are some of the considerations regarding mobile devices and some of the differences compared to laptop/desktop computers.

- Handheld
  - Embedded system (does only one thing).
  - Active device.
  - Smaller onboard storage capacity.
  - Forensics is done in part by active imaging.
  - Operates on push technology.
- Computer
  - Requires file system on storage device.
  - Static device.
  - Large storage capacity.
  - Forensics is accomplished in part by bit stream imaging.

Mobile devices often have the ability to be modified or wiped remotely. This is a security feature, but it also can be used to destroy evidence and make it unrecoverable in an investigation. One way of removing this threat is to utilize Faraday technology such as a Faraday bag or a Faraday cage. Faraday technology traces its roots to the nineteenth century physicist Michael Faraday. He discovered that an electrical charge is carried on the exterior surface of a conductor and that the charge had no influence on anything contained within the conductor. By using this principle, a cell phone can be placed inside a Faraday device such as a Faraday cage or a Faraday bag and be prevented from receiving cell signal. Faraday bags are often sealed with Velcro, and care must be taken to ensure that a proper seal is made in order to establish a signal shield. Figure 5.1 shows a picture of a Faraday bag.

An investigator should be aware that a powered on cellular device placed in a Faraday container may begin searching for service. This can drain battery life quickly. Placing the device in an airplane mode can help minimize the battery drain. Connecting the device to a charger by running a cable through an opening in the Faraday container can act like an antenna, which would establish signal connection and defeat the purpose of the Faraday container. It is possible to connect a self-contained trickle charger to the phone to help maintain battery life and place both the phone and the charger in the Faraday container. Figure 5.2 shows a picture of a trickle charger.

Figure 5.1   Blackberry on a Faraday bag.

Figure 5.2   Cell phone connected to trickle charger.

One of the complexities with investigating mobile devices and cell phones is the variety of information sources and figuring out how they fit together. Some of the sources of evidence in mobile devices are as follows:

- Provider/carrier
  - Pen link register—call detail, IMSI (subscriber ID), IMEI (equipment ID), and PIN/PUK (personal ID number/personal unlock key)
- Phone
  - Calls, SMS, MMS, and media (graphics, audio/video, and pictures)
- SIM card
  - Text messages, phone numbers (typically no graphics)
- Media card (graphics, audio/video, and pictures)

Typical provider information includes originating and terminating phone numbers, IMEI, initiating and terminating towers, service type, service date/time, and length of service/call. An investigator should verify the information before submitting their report.

An investigator must also have an understanding of how cell phones work. Radio waves connect the cell phone to a tower, and the tower connects the cell to the rest of the network. Higher frequency towers are closer together than lower frequency towers. It is important to note that frequency bands for cell usage may vary by country, so this may impact device configuration and capabilities.

When a caller turns a cell phone on, it listens for service. When a caller is traveling while utilizing the service, the signal is handed off to different towers along the route. Two common types of signal handoff between towers include a hard handoff and a soft handoff. A hard handoff is used by GSM technology, and the call is handled in a "break before make" manner. Essentially, the initial tower that has the call tells the next tower that it is giving it a call, and then the initial tower breaks service and assumes the second tower picked up servicing of the call. In a soft handoff, which is used by CDMA, a call is handled in a "make before break" manner. The initial tower informs the next tower that a call is being handed off, but in this environment, the initial tower waits until the second tower is servicing the call before breaking its connection with the call.

The generations of cell technology include 1G, 2G, 2.5G, 3G, and 4G. The G that follows each number represents generation. So 1G is first generation, 2G is second generation, and so on. Some of the aspects that characterize each generation are as follows:

- 1G
  - Frequency division
- 2G
  - Time division (going away)
  - Digital voice and improved data
  - iDEN (Nextel push to talk) and CDMA (Verizon)
- 2.5G
  - Enhanced Data rates for GSM Evolution (EDGE)
- 3G
  - Always on data access and live streaming video
- 4G
  - On-demand high-quality audio/video

Digital Cell Phone Investigation

The first step to any forensic investigation is to make sure that you have the authority to initiate the investigation. Laws and rationale for an investigation vary, and ethical practices should always be a primary objective. What is legal and what is ethical are not always the same thing, and an investigator needs to consider both aspects carefully. Once this is answered, the investigator should plan the investigation. Cell phones are often passcode protected, so if a phone is active, it should remain in active state if there is any question about being able to gain access if the device were to be turned off. However, remote wiping is a concern, so the device should be placed in a Faraday bag to prevent wiping from occurring. The device will be searching for signal when it is in a Faraday bag, so it may quickly wear down the battery. Hooking the phone up to a trickle charger while in the bag can eliminate this concern—and remembering the phone charger for later use can help avert charging issues down the road. Checking the device settings to make sure that it does not revert to protected mode is also a prudent precaution.

The steps to investigate a cell phone incident have many similarities to computer investigations, but there are also some distinct differences. Mobile forensic tools often have distinct logical and physical image extract options, and some tools also have file system extract utilities. Cell phone hardware and software are not consistent between vendors and among models, and the examiner often needs to modify the state of the phone before extracting information. This is usually done by altering the phone settings and allowing USB connectivity, enabling Bluetooth, or some other similar configuration. This permits the forensic tool to extract information from the device using a USB cable or Bluetooth connection. Figure 5.3 shows a cell phone connected to a Cellebrite UFED.

Cell phones often have media cards and SIM cards, which are additional sources of information. A common location for serial number and model information is on a sticker underneath the battery. Since maintaining power is often an issue, use of a search engine to find images of a phone is often a preferred way of determining model information. After the investigation is complete, the battery can be removed and the model information can be verified.

Figure 5.3   Cell phone connected to Cellebrite UFED.

Some forensic tools, such as Cellebrite, attempt to support as many devices as possible. Other forensic tools such as Katana's Lantern focus on a targeted environment such as Apple iOS devices and Androids. This specialization can allow the vendor to go deeper in its forensic analysis and provide more detailed analysis. Figure 5.4 shows an analysis of an iPad by Lantern.

Although mobile forensic tools often generate a detailed report, documenting the device and circumstances around the device should still be done. Similar to forensically processing a computer, mobile device investigation is well served by using a seizure form such as the one shown in Figure 5.5.

This form, developed by Det. Rebecca MacArthur, not only documents the device, it also helps document the investigation. The reason this is beneficial is that multiple tools may be used in a forensic examination, so keeping track of what types of analysis and which tools have been used can become difficult. A seizure form that assists in documenting an investigation in addition to the seizure itself can reduce errors and omissions.

Open source tools are commonly used in mobile forensics. There are some tools that are fairly extensive, as well as tools that serve a niche. Open source tools can provide a good way to verify the results and gain additional information. It is important that the forensic examiner be aware of the status of the tools and if it has been validated for legal situations. Tools that have not been validated and are used in investigations can have a negative impact on the case.

Cell forensic tools generally have extract reports built into the forensic extract process. They can also create formatted files that can be ported to other tools for further analysis. Cell towers and location information can then be visualized in tools such as Google Earth, and usage data can be further analyzed with tools such as i2 and THREADS. This type of analysis goes a step beyond just recovering raw data and utilizes visual analysis and statistical analysis to generate intelligence that is more actionable and may provide a larger perspective on what is occurring.

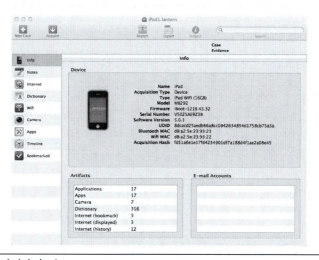

Figure 5.4   iPad analysis by Lantern.

Seizure Form for Phones (it is recommended to obtain charger for phone and to ask for passcode)		
Case Number\File Class	Authority to look at contents ☐ Search Warrant ☐ Consent	Evidence and or Tag #
Seized by\Date	Specific location found (if found on person – name)	
Phone Number (if known)\Statements made regarding who and how many people use the phone (include name, screen names, email addresses, nick names)		
Carrier\Brand Name	Color\Condition	
Is phone locked? What is passcode or pattern? (Do not attempt to unlock phone if password is not known. More than two attempts may disable phone permanently)		

Remove Battery for Phone Identifiers	
Model #	Serial Number
DEC	HEX
SIM Card(s)? If empty slot – ask owner if one was used and the whereabouts ID numbers on SIM(s)	SD card? If empty slot – ask owner if one was used and the whereabouts

Abilities of Phone
☐ Internet ☐ Text Msgs ☐ Camera ☐ Video ☐ Wi-Fi ☐ Hotspot ☐ Bluetooth ☐ GPS ☐ Other

Cell Phone Extraction Software (block phone from receiving service, Wi-Fi turned off)	
Software Used or Attempted	
Extractions successful ☐ Normal ☐ File System Dump ☐ Physical Dump ☐ Acquisition Notes:	Extractions not successful ☐ Normal ☐ File System Dump ☐ Physical Dump ☐ Acquisition Notes:

Items Extracted
☐ Contacts ☐ Incoming Calls ☐ Outgoing Calls ☐ Missed Calls ☐ Text Msgs ☐ Images ☐ Videos ☐ Other

Reports created\Location archived

Phone Number (viewed natively)

Other items viewed natively (Photograph or take Video)

Figure 5.5   Mobile device seizure form.

SD Card (if applicable) (remove and attach to Computer using Write Blocker)					
Software Used Thumbscrew\M2Cfg	☐ FTK Imager	☐ Xnview	☐ Faststone	☐ Encase	☐ Other
Previewed Date\Drive Number\Size listed on Card	Acquired Date\Name of Evidence File\Location archived\Actual size of Card\File System on Card				
Notes of Items of Interest:					
Title\Name\Date\Case Number					

Figure 5.5 (*Continued*) Mobile device seizure form.

Tools such as THREADS can analyze calling patterns, using attributes such as who initiated the call, the length of the call, frequency of calls between individuals, and when various people are called to determine who has leadership roles in a potential ring and the probability certain events are related. For example, if Jim calls Jane for 1 minute and then Jim calls Steve 30 seconds after ending the call with Jane—and this pattern is repeated a few times during a month—the likelihood that the calls between Jim and Jane and the calls between Jim and Steve are related is very high. On the other hand, if Jim calls Jane for 1 minute and then Jim calls Steve the day after calling Jane, the likelihood that the calls between Jim and Jane and the calls between Jim and Steve are related is much lower. This type of analysis can place people inside or outside the ring of likely suspects.

One of the most important attributes to focus on when examining mobile devices is when things occur. Temporal analysis of just cell phone activity by itself may not be enough to explain a situation, but when the analysis is augmented with the information from other sources on the same timeline chart, a more complete and compelling picture of what has occurred is often possible. The point being that a forensic cell phone extract may be useful, but combining it with visual analysis capabilities usually provides far more useful intelligence that can be used to impact a larger situation. The use of link and visual analysis in digital forensics is covered in more detail in Chapter 13.

Geographic Positioning Systems

A GPS utilizes coordinates from satellites to establish position and potential travel routes. Advances in smartphones have incorporated GPS applications and capabilities into one device, which has had a significant impact on the stand-alone GPS market. Routes, waypoints, and other information generated during the use of GPS technology can be useful in an investigation. There may be addresses, favorites, recent GPS coordinates, and configuration files that provide details of interest.

Cameras

Digital cameras include metadata in the picture file that provides additional information about the picture. This can include the camera name and model, as well as GPS coordinates of where the picture was taken. Most of the relevant information from a camera would be on media cards, though some cameras provide for additional extraction using interfaces such as USB. A camera is a potentially important aspect of a computer crime and should be seized with the computer. If no media card is present, the investigator should take a picture on a blank media card to obtain metadata information for use in keyword searches.

Video cameras are also sources of information for a digital forensic examiner. Video cameras often have large storage capacity—perhaps even a hard drive. As with a computer, the investigator should review the storage media for deleted files. Video camera forensics may be better suited for computer forensic tools rather than mobile forensic tools because the recovery capabilities of computer forensic tools tend to be more mature than those found in mobile forensic tools.

Summary

The need for mobile forensics is growing at a rapid rate due to the number of mobile devices in use and the expanding capabilities that they offer. Smartphones and tablets are popular platforms for a number of applications, which can provide additional evidence in a forensic investigation. Mobile forensics is an environment that requires a large number of tools and techniques to provide the most intelligence possible from a device. Forensic tools are often supplemented with visual analysis tools and geographic information systems to gain additional insight into an investigation.

Cellular Communications Technology Overview

Mobile technology is rife with acronyms, and the following are a few more that an investigator should be aware of

GSM—Global System for Mobile Communications. It is the standard digital cellular communications technology worldwide. It is found in more than 160 countries and is based off of TDMA.

TDMA—Time Division Multiple Access. TDMA was released in 1993 and quickly became the U.S. communication standard. It allows sustaining several data channels on a *single* frequency by assigning data streams specific time slots. There are six time slots for each frequency channel. Every conversation uses two time slots (one for each person). Information is sent in bursts and reassembled at the receiving end.

EDGE—Enhanced Data rate for GSM Evolution. It is a 3G technology that allows GSM carriers to use GSM radio bands for IP-based multimedia services and applications.

CDMA—Code Division Multiple Access. It is far more efficient than GSM or TDMA because of its better network capacity. It is a 2G technology that digitizes multiple conversations and breaking them into bits, attaching a code known only by the sender and the receiver, and then reassembling them. There are no time slots. Verizon—no SIM card and will not work outside United States. Spread spectrum—channels are spread across the "entire frequency" instead of dedicating to one. No hard limit to the number of users who may share one base.

PCS—Personal Communication Service. It does not support 900 band GSM phones.

ESN—Electronic Serial Number. It is primarily used in CDMA networks and identifies the device to the network. The MEID is an evolution of the ESN.

IMEI—International Mobile Equipment Identity. It is primarily used on GSM networks and identifies the device to the network.

IMSI—International Mobile Subscriber Identity. It identifies the subscriber to the network.

MEID—Mobile Equipment Identifier. It is primarily used in CDMA networks and identifies the device to the network. The MEID was created to replace the ESN.

SIM card—Subscriber Identity Module card. The IMSI is contained within the SIM card. The SIM card is the identification number for the GSM device, and also contains a secret user key, authentication algorithm (A3), and an encryption algorithm (A8). In addition to the network information, SIM cards may contain the address book, text messages, and the last several dialed numbers. Note that it may be illegal to clone a SIM card without proper authorization. Figure 5.6 shows a picture of a SIM card.

Figure 5.6 SIM card.

MSC—Mobile Switching Center. It connects subscribers to the network and other subscribers via switching functions.

MTSO—Mobile Phone Switching Office. It handles communication. Also note that MTSO checks to make sure phone is not stolen.

SMS—Short Message Service. It uses the SMS system, not GSM or MTSO.

MMS—Media Messaging Service.

iDEN—Integrated Digital Enhanced Network. Nextel push to talk.

References

Jansen, W., and Ayers, R. (2007). Guidelines on cell phone forensics. National Institute of Standards and Technology. Retrieved on July 10, 2011 from http://csrc.nist.gov/publications/nistpubs/800-101/SP800-101.pdf.

Owen, P., and Thomas, P. (2011). An analysis of digital forensic examinations: mobile devices versus hard disk drives utilizing ACPO and NIST guidelines. *Digital Investigations.* doi:10.1016/j.diin.2011.03.002.

Paul, I. (2011). Why Apple tracks you via iPhone: It's not what you think. Retrieved on January 25, 2012 from http://www.pcworld.com/article/225845/why_apple_tracks_you_via_iphone_its_not_why_you_think.html.

6

CLOUD COMPUTING AND DIGITAL FORENSICS

PROF. GERALD EMERICK

Introduction

Last week you received a meeting invitation from a manager in one of your organization's most critical and sensitive areas. The meeting seems to be related to a routine software vendor visit, and the manager is looking for someone to represent the information security team. You think to yourself, "No problem, I have done this a hundred times over the years." Ten minutes into the meeting, you realize the vendor only offers their application as a cloud service, and the organizational area is extremely excited by the cloud provider's claims of speed of delivery, ease of implementation, customer control, and minimal internal information systems requirements. The application will contain some of the organization's most sensitive data. The vendor finishes their presentation and opens the discussion for questions. Everyone looks pleased, and then the focus turns to you and there is an awkward silence. Perhaps you should have done your homework on cloud architecture, service models, deployment models, and security implications.

It has become impossible to attend a conference, review your e-mail inbox, read a technical magazine, or visit a popular information technology website without encountering an article or a presentation on cloud computing. Cloud computing is getting a lot of attention. Foregoing a formal definition for a moment, "cloud" really refers to the outsourcing of Internet-based infrastructures and applications to external service providers typically leveraging a high degree of virtualization. The long-term cost-saving claims of cloud computing as championed by the vendors are compelling to any chief information officer (CIO) or chief financial officer (CFO). Since Amazon launched cloud services targeting at the enterprises in 2008, this area of computing has continued to quickly gain attention. Given the compelling promises of financial savings, it appears as if this model of computing is here to stay. However, cloud computing and services are still very new to the world of information technology and as such the terminology, service offerings, and impact on current processes, people, and technology are still evolving, as well as the general knowledge of this new area of computing.

We will be taking a close look at challenges, risks, and benefits of cloud services in a moment, but first, it is prudent to establish a working definition of cloud computing, the common service offerings, and the delivery models as a foundation for the discussion. The most widely accepted, general definition of cloud computing comes from the National Institute of Standards and Technology (NIST). NIST defines cloud computing as "Cloud computing is a model for enabling ubiquitous, convenient, on-demand network access to a shared pool of configurable computing resources (e.g., networks, servers, storage, applications, and services) that can be rapidly provisioned and released with minimal management effort or service provider interaction. This cloud model is composed of five essential characteristics, three service models, and four deployment models."

With cloud computing, customers are in the control of their computing resource needs and can add computing resources as they wish through a highly automated and responsive set of processes. These automated processes do not typically require interaction with other people, and the turnaround time for adding new computing resources is very rapid. Envision an Internet web application that the customer can sign in to and add computing resources in minutes. These characteristics alone are appealing if only from a general customer service perspective. I cannot tell you how many times I have waited weeks and months for internal procurement, installation, and configuration processes so that the different phases of a new information system project could be executed. Consider the flexibility it provides a customer to quickly add computing resources so that a heavy load can be placed on their applications during a test cycle to validate that the applications can handle the peak shopping season. If these computing resources were internal, additional servers, operating systems, and system software may need to be purchased, installed, and configured just to support this test, and then the resources may sit idle until the peak season rolls around the next time. You may have noticed that I did not mention the term "multitenancy" or "virtualization" when describing the cloud characteristics, as these are the two terms that are often associated with cloud computing. Although these are common characteristics, they are not a requirement.

As our next step to building our cloud computing foundation, let us take a closer look at the three service models and four deployment models referenced in the NIST definition. Cloud services are generally categorized into three service models: (1) infrastructure as a service (IAAS), (2) platform as a service (PASS), and (3) software as a service (SASS); and four deployment models: (1) public, (2) private, (3) hybrid, and (4) community. One of the keys to understanding the differences between these models is to analyze the service models from the customer's perspective, specifically how much control, responsibility, and visibility the customer has over the operating system, applications, and system software such as the web server and database server. We will take a closer look at these three service models in a moment. The four cloud deployment models are briefly described as follows:

1. *Public:* Services are used over the network or Internet. All infrastructures except for basic networking components are located at the cloud provider. In addition, the operating system, system software, and applications are deployed and managed within the cloud provider's infrastructure at one or more of the cloud provider's data centers.

2. *Private:* Infrastructures and applications are hosted internally but offer some of the same benefits of cloud computing such as ability to shrink or expand the computing power and capacity on demand. Customers who are uncomfortable with placing their data and process in a public cloud but still like the advantages of a flexible cloud configuration may find this option attractive. Government regulations and laws may also drive a customer to choose this model. Consider a government application with classified information that cannot be deployed to a multi-tenant model due to a customer's policy or law.

3. *Hybrid:* This model is a combination of public and private clouds. For some of the same reasons stated in the private deployment model, customers may choose or be forced due to policy or regulation to deploy part of their system internally yet still take advantage of a public cloud service for other components of their systems and applications.

4. *Community:* This model is really a hybrid of the hybrid model. This model may be public, private, or both, but what makes it a little different is the customers who use the cloud service are part of a "community" with shared interests, goals, missions, and so on.

Let us now take a closer look at the three different service models offered and their characteristics.

Infrastructure as a Service

In this model, a virtual machine or server is provided to the customer. The customer has control over the operating system, storage, network configuration, and any application and system software such as web servers, database management systems, and network software including host-based firewalls. Customers can add processing power, virtual machines, and memory on demand. In this model, the customer is also responsible for the following:

- Operating system patches
- System software configuration
- Web server administration
- Database administration
- Patches to all system software
- Security implications including confidentiality, integrity, and availability related to not performing operating system, application software, and system software installation, configuration, and patching correctly

Platform as a Service

In this model, the customer selects an operating system environment, system software, and network configuration from the PAAS provider's offerings. The customer installs and configures applications, but the cloud provider is primarily responsible for the operating system and operating system patches, storage, and network configuration. The customer and cloud service provider may have shared responsibility for system software such as web servers and database management systems. The cloud service provider may be responsible for the installation and configuration of the system software, but the customer may have full administration rights including rights that may override the cloud provider's original, default configuration settings.

The customer has complete responsibility for the installation and configuration of business applications and for the creation and administration of website applications and data access. The customer may share some network responsibility such as choosing whether to make the DNS of the database publicly available to support remote connections from the applications not hosted by the cloud provider. The cloud provider will have responsibility for web server and database management system software patches and upgrades, and may control some of the administrative functions such as basic backup and recovery of databases and websites. The customers' ability to add processing power and memory may be limited by the cloud provider.

Software as a Service

In this model, the cloud provider has control over the operating system, system software, network configuration, storage, application installation, and configuration. Customers typically access an application using a web browser or minimal client software. Customer administrators may have role-based access to application administration features delivered through the SAAS application.

In the SAAS model, the ability to add more processing power through additional virtual machines, memory, or disk is not in the customer's control. This control is replaced by a service level agreement (SLA), which states availability and response times, between the SAAS provider and the customer. The SAAS provider may add virtual machines, processors, memory, or disk to ensure that the SLA is being met.

Application programming interfaces (APIs) may be available to interact with application processes and data including data extracts, data updates, and integrations. Integration may also be provided as a service by the SAAS provider or through a third-party integration service provider.

Service and Deployment Models

The boundaries around these deployment and service models can be a bit blurry. For example, it is possible to offer a public cloud deployment that is virtually private through the use of virtual private networks. Certainly, the distinction can be blurry between the hybrid and community models as well. The aforementioned deployment models and service models simply offer a framework in which services can be offered, consumed, and evaluated. Since the public model is the most popular deployment model and SAAS pushes much of the direct security responsibility to the cloud provider, we focus much of our discussion on the public deployment model and the SAAS

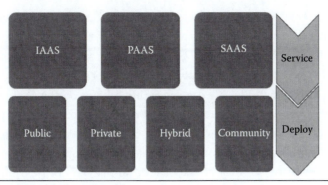

Figure 6.1 Cloud service and deployment models.

service model. Figure 6.1 depicts the types of cloud architectures and their service and deployment options.

Customer versus Cloud Provider Responsibilities

As you move from the IAAS to PAAS to SAAS service models, the control that the customer has over the configuration of the operating system and other system software such as web servers and database servers diminishes. This control diminishes to the point where in the SAAS model the customer interacts with the cloud service completely through an abstract application delivered via a browser or an API. The customer may not be aware of or even care what operating system, web server, or database server is hosting the SAAS application.

As shown in Figure 6.2, each successive service model builds on the features of the previous model. PAAS uses infrastructure services from IAAS, and SAAS uses operating systems and system software from PAAS. In the SAAS model, the infrastructure,

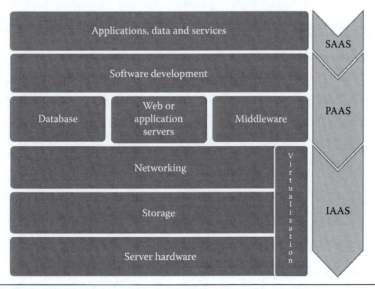

Figure 6.2 Application stack by service models.

operating system software is all abstracted from a customer's view. However, the IAAS and PAAS layers still exist; they are just managed by the SAAS provider. Given this model, there is nothing that prevents a SAAS provider from using the services of a separate IAAS or PAAS service provider. From a customer's perspective, the closer you are to using a SAAS service model, the more you are relying on the cloud service provider to offer a secure and reliable solution. The closer the customer is to the IAAS service model, the more responsibility the customer is taking on in terms of providing a secure and reliable solution. However, the customer also maintains more control over their data and processes. With this control comes responsibility. In both extremes, all security concerns need to be addressed by SLA contracts in the SAAS model or by building and implementing the customer's security policies and solutions in the IAAS model.

In the SAAS service model, isn't the customer still ultimately responsible for a secure and reliable solution? Yes, they are relying on the SAAS service provider to maintain their SLAs, but the customer cannot transfer all risks and accountability to the cloud service provider.

Other Service Models

There are additional cloud service models that do not necessarily fit nicely into one of these categories. One example of these models is integration as a service. We have an immediate problem with this model as it shares the same acronym as "infrastructure as a service" (IAAS)! The integration as a service model provides an integration between customer legacy systems and the SAAS application as well as integration between separate SAAS applications in the cloud. These integration service providers may offer prebuilt software integration adapters that speed up the integration process to popular legacy customer enterprise resource planning (ERP) systems or other SAAS applications that are likely related within the same business process. For example, perhaps a human resources SAAS provider has partnered with a payroll SAAS provider and uses integration as a service provider to perform the integration (data movement and transformation) between their human resources application and the most popular SAAS payroll applications. This presents customers with more external options to implement and integrate a complete solution and also even more security concerns as you are introducing yet another public service layer into your solution. Not only do you have to evaluate the SAAS provider but now you have to do the same detailed evaluation for the integration provider. Furthermore, who is in control and responsible for the interfaces when you use an integration service provider? When does the SAAS provider upgrade their applications that are responsible for the interface impact? How much visibility do you have as a customer into the interfaces provided by the integration service provider? How do you know the interfaces are secure if you are not initiating, administering, and monitoring these interfaces? Can you really trust the SAAS provider and the integration service provider to represent your best interest as a customer? Some of the integration service providers I have evaluated let the customer maintain control over changes to the interfaces.

In this model, you are using the integration service provider's infrastructure and software components to quickly configure and administer your integrations. You as a customer control changes and deployment of the interfaces. However, in the spirit of customer service, the service provider may offer to do this for the customer. A balance must be struck between the speed of implementation, long-term flexibility, data quality, and risk.

Another concern with this model is the ability of the customer to migrate to a different SAAS provider. Returning to our human resources example above, if the customer chose to migrate to a different payroll SAAS provider, they may have to involve the human resources SAAS provider and the integration as a services provider, both of which are external to their organization. Would the integration as a service provider limit the customer's choices of payroll providers? Would the human resources SAAS provider need to modify their interfaces to the integration service provider? The answer to both of these questions, given the maturity of these offerings, is likely "Yes." How do you ensure that all the data are properly destroyed at the previous payroll provider's facility after migration? Contracts between the customer and the cloud provider must address these concerns. In addition, it is likely that the customer would need some of the same interface components for their internal systems resulting in duplication of the human resource interface components. This would certainly impact financial incentives and could result in data quality and consistency problems. In this scenario, how many places are we now storing, transferring, and processing the data? Initial implementations may result in data and process at more locations than the customer would like to have or perhaps did before migrating to the cloud service. This certainly increases the complexity of incident response and digital forensics processes.

Integration requirements do not go away in a SAAS model. In fact, they may become much more complicated as your integration must likely occur securely over a public network. In addition, not all SAAS services are created equal. Some offer sophisticated programming APIs, whereas others only offer basic import and export of some of the data. It is not uncommon to have more custom integrations in the SAAS implementation project. These integrations may present several security risks:

1. Data at rest may need to be encrypted.
2. Data in motion will certainly need to be encrypted across the network.
3. Private and public keys used for encryption must be managed internally and externally at the cloud provider.
4. You will need to rely on your SLA with the cloud provider to ensure confidentiality, integrity, and availability of your data.

In Figure 6.3, we can see how the integration service provider may have the ability to initiate data import and export, execute remote processes, and transfer files. Any one of these processes may result in temporary or permanent data resident within the integration as a service's infrastructure. Consider the complexity of auditing the movement of this data and transformation from the SAAS provider to the integration provider, to the customer, back to the integration provider, and then out to one more

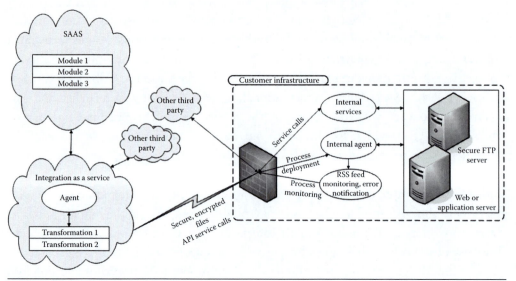

Figure 6.3 Integration as a service.

SAAS providers including the originating SAAS provider. Security professionals need to ensure that the data is secure during all these operations whether the data is at rest, in process, or in transfer. Customers should proceed with caution if they decide to take the integration as a service approach as they are placing a lot of trust in their service providers to represent their long-term interests.

Multi-Tenancy

If there is one cloud buzzword that gets the attention of a security-minded information technology manager, it is "multi-tenancy." Multi-tenancy is one of the drivers of the economies of scale that make cloud service offerings financially attractive and enables the cloud service provider to manage their operations efficiently. What does multi-tenancy really mean? The meaning and implementation can change quite drastically in each of the service and deployment models. For example, in an IAAS model, your hardware will be shared in a multi-tenant manner with other customers, but your operating systems and system software may not. In PAAS, your operating system and system software may be shared with other customers, but your applications are not. As you move from IAAS to PAAS to SAAS, the amount of multi-tenancy will increase. In SAAS, it is not uncommon to share the same physical database instance with other customers. Your data may be comingled in the same tables as your competitors! Let us hope the cloud database administrator does not accidently modify a database view or security group incorrectly that allows customers to briefly see each other's data! Furthermore, a successful SQL injection attack may reveal data from multiple customers in this model. Let us think about this SQL injection attack for a moment. In a SQL injection attack, the attacker "tricks" the application into executing the database queries that have been written by the attacker and injected into the web application input fields. In a successful attack on a multi-tenant SAAS service model, these injected queries could potentially result in data being displayed to the attacker from multiple customers or customer data being modified inappropriately across the customer boundaries. You may be thinking "sure, but they'll only see data at their privilege level." This is probably not going to be the case. Most web applications are architected in such a way that the account that accesses the database is a privileged account, separate from the account the user logged into the SAAS application with. When there are hundreds of thousands of users accessing a web application, it is often not feasible or desirable to maintain individual user accounts and privileges at the database level. Instead, the web or application server will assign the user role-based access to the application and then connect to the database with a single privileged account on behalf of all the users. In an SQL injection attack you are leveraging the same privileged database account and, therefore, likely will have access to the entire database.

SAAS salespeople are very proud of their large customers who use their software and do not hesitate to advertise these large customers as a means of endorsement. A list of the SAAS provider's large customers would not be hard to find by the attacker. Some companies and organizations are more of a target of an attack than others. Should customers view high-profile customers who use the same SAAS service as a threat since they invite attacks or a resounding endorsement for the product? I would think most customers would not want to share a multi-tenant database with a popular attack target.

Customers in a multi-tenant environment using the IAAS or PAAS models cannot be trusted to build and deploy applications that are free of vulnerabilities. Therefore, a proper segregation of customer applications, data, and administrative privileges is critical. Sharing operating system accounts across the customers should not be possible. Database instances and accounts should be separated as well. Ideally, each customer should have their own database instance with separate access accounts that implement the principles of least privilege. Separate access accounts are common. However, separate database instances are not and may be counter to the cloud provider's economies of the scale model. Trust boundaries between application architecture tiers become much more complicated in a multi-tenant environment. Not only do the application architecture tiers need to establish general trust boundaries with one another, also the trust boundaries need to be established that are customer specific within each application architecture tier.

User Access and Provisioning

SAAS applications must appeal to a broad range of customer capabilities when it comes to managing users, user groups, and authentication and authorization process. The SAAS application will likely offer the ability to create users, groups, and permissions directly in the application to avoid alienating the customers who are not willing to invest in an integration to their identity management system. Customers must have a strategy for managing this user and privilege information separate from their organization's central identity management or must be prepared to integrate with their central identity management systems. Manually maintaining users, groups, and privileges in a separate system presents many challenges. Auditing, on-boarding, and off-boarding employee processes may become a challenge. User data used for authentication and authorization can easily become out of synchronization with the customer's central identity management system. Ensuring employees who have left the organization are removed from the SAAS application in a timely manner may become a challenge. Updating user privileges as their role in the organization changes may be a challenge as well. A process to audit the users and permissions may have to be custom built by the customer using the cloud provider's API. Whether the process is manual or automated, there may be an unacceptable lag time for removing the users from the SAAS system that requires a manual process in some circumstances.

Some SAAS providers offer different forms of single sign-on (SSO). The SSO process allows the users who have been authenticated to the customer's network to "automatically" authenticate to the SAAS application. Customers should investigate whether a SAAS application allows a configuration of SSO and direct authentication simultaneously. In some instances, I have seen the customer forced to choose one or the other but not both. It may be possible and desirable for a customer to implement SSO, but it presents a number of challenges as well. SSO is primarily an end-user convenience as it eliminates the end user from being prompted to log in a second time after they have already authenticated to the customer's network. Implementing SSO reduces the number of passwords and log-ins for the end user but does not necessarily eliminate manual maintenance or the need for a custom interface to the SAAS application. The user identities and group permissions must still be synchronized between the customer and the SAAS application.

In cases where the SAAS application is accessible from the Internet without first signing into the customer's network, SSO is further complicated. The customer may have to have the SAAS provider redirect to a site managed by the customer, have the user authenticate to the customer's network, and then redirect with credentials passed to the SAAS application. This not only introduces more points of failure and confusion to the end user but also a larger attack surface for an attacker bent on accessing the SAAS application. Other scenarios that complicate SSO with SAAS providers include shared computers within the customer's network. It is not uncommon for employees in a manufacturing area to share a common, kiosk style computer that is connected to the network with a common user account and password when the computer boots. The employees may be prompted to log in to certain applications and then must remember to log out before leaving the shared computer. Similar to the previous Internet access scenario, the SSO integration must accommodate these employees as well even if the shared computers to do not support SSO to the SAAS provider. The complexity of the integration and the attack surface increases further as does the complexity of auditing and monitoring of employee access to the SAAS application.

Customers will need to adopt standard identity management practices and interfaces as they move toward cloud computing. It is not sustainable to build custom integrations for each cloud provider. Standards such as Service Provisioning Markup Language (SPML) are emerging but to date have not been widely accepted due to complexity and investment requirements. Today, a customer would have to write a provisioning service for implementation of each cloud provider's SPML. This results in a standard method of provisioning but does not reduce the complexity or the number of interfaces that need to be maintained by the customer and the cloud provider. A standard provisioning interface such as SPML would provide basic user data operations such as read, update, create, or delete using a standard extensible markup language (XML) schema. The standard service may also provide basic user data search operations. Other open standards such as OpenID, Yahoo!, and Google enable SSO and authentication to a cloud service provider. However, the control of user accounts and passwords used in these standards are out of the customer's control and, therefore, present their own set of risks and challenges.

Data Protection and Breaches

A common defense and customer requirement in a cloud environment requires encryption of data when in transit and at rest. I do not disagree with this practice. Any data in transit on the network and at rest should be encrypted. Encrypting the data can help protect against other customers or cloud provider employees from compromising data confidentiality. The encryption method used should be deemed acceptable according to the customer's industry or government's policies and recommendations. However, this defense provides limited protection when a web application is compromised. For example, if the SAAS application authentication is bypassed or compromised, the SAAS application architecture components may view requests for data as legitimate, allowing the attacker to view the encrypted data in an unencrypted form. Furthermore, some data encryption implementations only guard against a stolen disk drive. In this situation, anyone with legitimate or compromised access to the database may view the data in an unencrypted form as the database engine may automatically unencrypt the data if the user has access privileges to the database.

In all these three cloud service models, the customer has complete (IAAS or PAAS) or shared (SAAS) responsibility for the encryption of their data and the management of the encryption keys. Customers must analyze and understand how the cloud provider is protecting their data. Simply stating that "we encrypt all data" is not a sufficient answer. This must include a review of how the cloud provider manages the encryption keys including how keys are generated, where the keys are stored, how access is controlled, and who has access to the encryption keys. The customer should also be aware of how the encryption keys might be shared within the SAAS provider's application architecture across the customers. Customers may choose to have a third party manage the encryption keys as a means of mitigating the risk.

The location of application processes and data are certainly strongly influenced by the cloud provider type and model. However, even in the SAAS model, it is likely that when viewing the entire business solution, application processes and data are scattered internally within the customer's infrastructure and externally at the cloud service provider. In a large organization, it is very uncommon to be able to relocate application processes and data that support the business process in their entirety. Inevitably, any significant business application will need to share the data and process with other business applications that may be external at a different cloud or service provider or hosted internally at the customer's location. At a minimum, most customers will need the data from all significant business applications in a data warehouse where the data can be combined with other areas of the business for analysis. This data consolidation and analytical reporting is typically not performed in the cloud, at least not yet. Knowing the location of the application processes and data is critical to understanding vulnerabilities, where audit and logging should and will occur, and encryption requirements. Physical location of data and application processes may not be known in a cloud model. In a multi-tenant model, multiple data centers acting as hot backups to each other may be part of the solution resulting in sensitive data in multiple locations.

Data import processes from the customer to the cloud provider may introduce opportunities for cross-site scripting attacks. In some cross-site scripting attacks, the goal is to insert some HTML or JavaScript code into a web page. To get the HTML or JavaScript into the web page, the application must accept the HTML or JavaScript and store it to the application's database. When the web application renders the web page, including the inserted HTML or JavaScript, the site has been compromised resulting in possible defacement of the site or other potentially malicious activities such as an attempt to steal a user's web application session. Traditionally, this type of cross-site scripting attack has occurred directly within web applications that do not properly validate the user input entered through an Internet browser. I have described scenarios where internal users, internal systems, and third-party integration as a service provider may be extracting, transforming, transmitting, and importing data. Any of these processes and responsible parties introduces an opportunity for an attacker to compromise the data including a potentially successful cross-site scripting attack through the insertion of HTML and JavaScript in the data being processed. Application vulnerability scanners will be of no use finding this type of cross-site scripting vulnerability. This does not mean that application vulnerability assessments should not be executed against the cloud provider's application. The cloud provider should regularly execute an application vulnerability scanner against their applications. Customers may want to receive contractual permission from the cloud provider to run their own vulnerability scanner against the application.

Operating system access resulting from a data breach should be a concern as well. Some of the large, popular database vendors allow privileged access to the operating system during a database operation such as data query or update. This feature should be turned off for obvious reasons. However, if the SAAS application was architected to require operating system access for some operations, this may present a vulnerability to all the customers who share the database server instance. SQL injection attacks can exploit this vulnerability by implicitly executing operating system commands through the injected SQL. These commands can be anything from moving files, deleting files, or scanning files on the operating system. Customers should inquire about database instance configuration settings and require that the database be configured in a secure manner.

Data security and protection laws may vary by country. In particular, the European Union has data privacy laws that can cause grief for global organizations attempting to leverage not only a global SAAS implementation but an implementation that may involve an integration as a service provider. Any party that processes the data must adhere to a country's data privacy laws. A process that is completely acceptable in the United States may be unacceptable and potentially against the law in a European country. As an example, temporarily writing unecrypted data to disk during an extraction, transformation, and load process may violate data privacy agreements and prevent part of the SAAS solution from being deployed in a data center closest to the end user or force the customer to perform parts of the extraction, transformation, and load process themselves.

Data breaches are at the top of the security concerns of cloud computing. The thought of having sensitive data comingled on shared database server instances or perhaps even in the same database as other customers make information technology managers squeamish. Anyone who has worked in information technology as a database administrator knows that it only takes a few errant clicks or accidental cascading privilege changes to give permissions where one did not intend to. For these reasons and others, all sensitive data in the cloud should not only be encrypted at rest and in transit but also be completely understood from the extraction, transformation, and load perspectives at all relevant locations in the application architecture including third parties, internal systems, and internal users. Encryption keys should not be shared between the customers, and the management of the encryption keys must be understood and agreeable to the customers.

Information Technology and Information Security Governance and Change Control Processes

If customers do not have mature information technology and information security governance processes in place, they are very vulnerable to adopting a cloud service without understanding or managing the risks. In my experience, SAAS providers tend to market to areas of the customer other than information technology, claiming that one of the big benefits of SAAS is that you do not need much of your information technology and information security staff's time. They may claim to offer a point-and-click configuration: "just upload a data file and get started." Anyone who has been involved in the implementation and integration of information technology systems knows that it is never that easy. Encouraging the end users to simply upload data files or e-mail the files is reckless. Many information technology professionals do not understand the need and methods to properly encrypt and transfer data let alone the end users of the applications. Consider the additional risk that is presented when the end users are given the ability to upload and download sensitive data directly to and from a SAAS application. Is the data encrypted on the user's workstation? Is the data encrypted during the upload and download processes? If so, the data must be encrypted using the same standards and methods as approved and governed by the information security team including the management of private keys. Procedures for giving the end users administrative access to the SAAS application must be established such that consistent methods for data management and transmission can be followed. This may become increasingly difficult if administration responsibility is outside of traditional boundaries and visibility of the information security team.

Service Access Vulnerabilities

In all of these service models, the only client software from the customer who may be communicating with the cloud provider is a browser or perhaps a simple file transfer protocol (FTP) client. On the other hand, the cloud providers may make their system software available from traditional clients. For example, a PAAS provider may allow a customer to connect to a database server using the database vendor's client software. This allows the customer to take advantage of a full-featured administration and development toolset from the database vendor. This also introduces some security risks and will be described momentarily. When the PAAS providers allow the customers to connect to their database servers via database vendor's administration and development tools, it can subject the database servers to attacks (Figure 6.4).

Figure 6.4   Database directory.

Figure 6.4 is a snapshot of a client database development tool connecting to a PAAS-provided enterprise-level relational database. This does introduce vulnerabilities as the cloud provider is no longer in complete control of the software accessing their system software resources. In one example, the PAAS provider exposes a list of all databases installed on the server although the customer may only have access credentials to one of the databases. This encourages attacks on the databases that are not the customer's and gives an attacker some critical information as a starting point, the database name. It would not be unthinkable to have administrative accounts with a similar name to the database. In addition, the database name itself may offer a strong indication of the nature of the database or the organization associated with the database. In the example below, the customer has access to a single database. There are hundreds of databases on this server that do not belong to the customer but are visible by name to the customer. Brute-force attacks that use that database name as a starting point for user accounts and passwords are likely.

Using an FTP service to transmit and update application files is very common in the IAAS and PASS models. The FTP transfers data in an unencrypted format allowing anyone with access to the network the ability to sniff or view the traffic. Application files often include sensitive data such as database user accounts and passwords, file transfer user accounts and passwords, and network disk drive user accounts. Many development tools allow and, in fact, encourage, through default settings, the transfer of sensitive application files through FTP services built directly into the development tools. Developers and administrators should always use a secure file transfer program while transferring the application files.

Migration Planning

Cloud customers need to ensure that they have a cloud service migration plan including data migration should they choose to discontinue their current cloud service or switch to a new cloud service. This concern is most significant in the SAAS model where customers may have little access to their raw data as controlled by the SAAS application. One method of testing a cloud provider's ability to extract a customer's data is to present data warehousing requirements to the cloud provider to determine their capabilities to extract and transform the customer's data in the customer's specified format. Another sign of cloud service provider capabilities is how easily they can establish a development and test environment for the customer. Internally, this may be easy for the cloud provider if they have mature procedures to isolate, copy, and, hopefully, obfuscate sensitive data to a test or development environment. If the cloud provider appears to struggle with such a request, further investigation of the cloud provider's data migration capabilities should follow. Executing backups of the SAAS provider's data and restoring this data to an internal database provide some assurance as to the feasibility of a migration and recovery.

In any case, the customer must have the ability to obtain their data in a timely fashion to support a migration to a new SASS provider. Understanding the time required to extract, transfer, and load the data is a must. Data extraction may be complicated by the requirement for the customer to obtain data through the API. Customers should review the API for data export capabilities. Cloud provider APIs that do not provide "bulk" data extraction may result in custom, expensive data export processes when needed by the customer to migrate elsewhere. The customer should also thoroughly understand all data destruction activities that will occur at the previous cloud service provider.

Incident Response

Introducing cloud-based computing to an organization broadens the scope of the information security team's incident response processes. The customer should define incident notification procedures with the cloud provider including what is considered an incident, who will be notified, and when the notification must occur. The customer may need to partner with the cloud provider during an investigation. Ensure that the cloud provider's application and system logs can be obtained and analyzed by the customer before an incident occurs. The customer should also determine how quickly a cloud-based application can be shut down and restarted including access to the customer's data. If a data breach incident occurs, the security team may not be able to keep the incident internal to the organization and be forced to involve one or more cloud service providers. The organization's incident response team may have to track the incident from an employee's laptop where a personal, private encryption key may have been used, e-mail, or FTP out to one or more cloud service providers. Cloud service providers may then transfer data to other cloud service providers on behalf of the customer, or an intermediate cloud service acting as an integrator may pick up the data from the FTP server, transform it, and then transfer and load the data to one or more service providers. If this sounds like a nightmare, consider that there may not be fewer steps if all the applications were internal to the organization, and in fact, certain steps might be less secure since employees tend to trust data at rest and data in motion more when it resides internally.

Virtualization

Virtualization is strongly associated with cloud computing and typically forms the foundation by which the IAAS, PAAS, and SAAS models are deployed. The elasticity of the cloud is significantly enabled by virtualization and the associated agility for deploying and creating additional computer operating environments and configurations. In the IAAS model, customers may be allowed to create their own local virtual machine configurations and then deploy these virtual machines to the IAAS cloud provider. Similar to comingling customer data within the same database instance, customers should be aware of the multi-tenant or comingling aspects of their deployed virtual machines. Customers may be less prudent with hardening virtual machines that have lower security requirements. Therefore, virtual machines that contain highly sensitive applications and processes may need to be kept separate from virtual machines that do not for fear that less secure virtual machines may create an attack vector that could impact more security sensitive virtual machines. In addition, traditional network security may not completely apply to virtual machine configurations. Virtual machines may not be required to communicate with each other over the physical network that may render some network security devices and processes useless while attempting to monitoring traffic between virtual machines.

Security Benefits of Cloud

Are there actually security benefits of cloud computing? An argument can be made, especially in smaller organizations or organizations that have immature security policies, procedures, and resources, that cloud computing is more secure. Information security is complicated. Designing, developing, and deploying secure operating systems, networks, databases, and web applications is incredibly complicated and expensive. Leveraging a cloud provider that has expertise in information security can improve your organization's security posture. Consider a small, local credit union bank and the resources they do and do not have at their disposal from an information security perspective. Are they able to attract and maintain the talent necessary to implement and maintain secure computing systems and applications or might they be better off partnering with a cloud service provider that has a proven track record and a reputation on the line when it comes to security? Personally, this line of thinking is one of the primary reasons I use a third-party payment service on smaller e-commerce sites.

Moving an internal, critical application within an organization to a cloud provider might force an organization to finally deal with security issues that it has been able or willing to delay because the system is internal and, therefore considered, "not really a risk." It is well documented that many if not the majority of information security threats come from within an organization. Analyzing how to move a critical internal system to the cloud will certainly force an organization to scrutinize the entire system, its data, processes, and dependencies. SLAs are common and more often than not a requirement of cloud computing. The process of establishing an SLA with a cloud provider will force the customer to evaluate their internal policies and procedures. The customer will need to compute penalties for violations of the SLA. This process may result in recognition for better internal controls and policies to reduce the risk.

7

INCIDENT RESPONSE

DET. JASON OTTING

Introduction

Law enforcement is faced with many challenges in regard to crimes involving computer technology. Many of these crimes involve child exploitation, and digital forensics is central in bringing justice to these cases. The following case summary is such an example, and unfortunately the scenario is all too common. Reviewing a case such as this can assist investigators in preparation for similar situations.

Case Summary

By many accounts, John Doe was an upstanding citizen of the community with a longtime wife, two children, good job, and a family dog. As an IT director for a local school system, he presented as a professional and knowledgeable persona to those around him. He took his family on vacations as most fathers do and doted on his children. His hobbies included photography, which he shared with his children. No one knew the secrets and the evil that was done inside his home, not even his wife.

Doe became the subject of an investigation and later a conviction of sexually abusing his daughter from age 7 to 14, and was also found to be in possession of child pornography—some of which included his own child. After the dust settled, his other child came forward and informed authorities that she too had been a victim of sexual abuse. Doe's obsession had destroyed his family and the innocence of his own children, leaving in its wake a mother and two daughters to heal the emotional wounds caused by a predator in their own home.

The Initiation of an Investigation

Criminal investigations can start in a variety of ways. They can come from an anonymous tip called into a law enforcement office, sent in by mail, from the victims themselves or their friends, or a referral from a school. In this case, the latter applies. A friend of the victim informed a counselor at school and that counselor acted on the information by alerting authorities. In many cases, when victims are exposed to sexual abuse by a parent at such a young age, they are unaware that what they are being asked to do is wrong. They are manipulated and are told that it is an act of love and that it must remain a secret. Doe used this manipulation on his children and preyed on their innocence to act on his desires. It was only after Doe's daughter made a comment to a friend about having sex with her father that she learned that this was not something that all children did, and at this time was scared to tell anyone for the fear that no one would believe her and the fear of the pain the truth would bring to her mother. She confided to her closest friends who urged her to come forward and yet she could not. She was a prisoner in her own home, a place where a child should feel protected.

After the counselor was made aware of what she had confided to her friend, she contacted the detective whom she had worked with on other investigations. These resulted in very lengthy, detailed, and complicated investigations that resulted in successful prosecution of a dangerous predator.

Information

After the law enforcement is made aware of such an accusation where a child is still in danger of further abuse, there is an urgency to gather as much information as possible immediately. Such urgency is not always present in other criminal investigations involving property crimes or narcotics, where there is luxury of conducting surveillance and conducting background investigation. The urgency is necessary to protect the child and the steps taken must be done carefully and efficiently. In this case, the initial detective immediately went to the school to speak with the alleged victim who was expecting the law enforcement's arrival. The initial interview is an important one; it is to determine credibility. Therefore, as much specific information that can be obtained is extremely vital. This information, while it may be vile and difficult to talk about, is necessary. In the initial interview, the investigator asked about the types of abuse and incidents that she described to her friends. It is not only important to determine the manner in which the predator violates the victim, but also the locations, the method, and as many details that can be remembered. Although it may seem mundane and unimportant at the time, such details such as types of bedspreads or colors of the paint in the room can lead to vital evidence down the road. The victim described how her father would wait until their mother was asleep, and would come into her room and read her bedtime stories, lay with her, and begin to manipulate her vagina at first with his fingers and then penetrate it with his penis. She would also describe his use of a common household personal hygiene item that he would use on her to "help stimulate" her. The information gathered at this interview is used as a probable cause to draft a search warrant for the home and gain vital evidentiary items. The victim in this case also described how her father would show her pornography, some of which included children on his computer. She would describe what model computer it was, and that this was his attempt to peak her interest where he would later rape her.

Child predators will often show that they will act on the manifestations of their desires. In this case, Doe had shown his daughter pornography, so the presence of digital evidence is expected in the home. It was at this point, the lead investigator would enlist the assistance of another detective to collect all the evidence related to the possible possession and distribution of child pornography. Given the nature of Doe's employment, it was expected there would be an abundance of digital media, storage devices, camera equipment, and computers at the residence. The search warrant would not only include information related to the actual assaults, it would also include all items that electronic evidence can be stored on.

Evidence Gathering

The next step would involve the lead investigator using the information gathered during the initial interviews with the victim and her friends to write a search warrant to gather evidence from the home. Together with digital forensic investigators, the team would execute that warrant on the home. Again, given the nature of the crime and the relationship with the victim, time was of the essence and it must be done prior to the child being in danger of further assault or further manipulation from her father.

Prior to leaving to execute the search warrant, field kits are gathered. It is important to gather all the tools that you may need, such as screwdrivers, bags for evidence, and portable imaging hardware and software in the event that the suspect machine must be imaged in place. Evidence logs are also used to document what and where the evidence was seized. Gathering a proper field kit may take trial and error, but it is essential that cameras, logs, bags, software, and hardware tools are included.

Information suggested that the mother was not aware of the abuse and there were not concerns of destruction of the evidence, so the search warrant would not be conducted as they are typically depicted on Hollywood movie screens, where police are shown bursting through the door and taking over the home. It is done delicately and slowly, remembering there is more than one victim in this case. The family as a whole is a victim of a sexual predator, and the search warrant will come as a shock to the initial victim's mother. With this in mind, the investigators approach and politely ask to come in, so they may speak in private to explain the allegations and why they are there. Once inside the home, the mother of the victim is shown the search warrant, made aware of the information alleged, and interviewed by the lead investigator, while other officers begin to gather evidence and process the scene.

At the beginning, every scene should be treated the same, no matter what the crime. It is essential to photograph everything as it was in its original position prior to moving it or seizing it. If computers are left on, the screens are to be photographed with care taken to observe whether there is evidence of encryption. If possible, a RAM dump should be done to procure any information and possible evidence that still may be stored in the RAM. In this particular case, the suspect was not at home during the initiation of the search warrant and seizure of the evidence and the computers were taken as is. All power cords, flash drives, SD cards, camera equipment, iPods, and any device that can hold digital evidence were seized. In all, the suspect had regular access to not only his personal laptops, but the family desktop and other storage devices in the house, such as external hard drives. Doe was also an avid Apple user and was in possession of an iPhone, which investigators would also want to seize. Doe arrived home during the execution of the warrant and was escorted to the kitchen area where the lead investigator would tell him why they were there. Prior to that, his iPhone would be taken.

In all, there were 20 flash drives, 25 SD cards, 4 external hard drives, 2 laptops, and 1 desktop taken from the scene. In addition, the hygiene product described by the victim was also located and taken into evidence. Pictures of the scene were placed into evidence and, where possible, written statements were taken from those in the home. Statements may be made to aid prosecution.

Interviews and the Analysis of Evidence

Once Doe arrived home and was informed of the allegations in the kitchen, he was asked to come to the police station where he could be interviewed and questioned further. Whenever possible and if the suspects are cooperative, interviews should be conducted in a controlled environment where they can be videotaped and away from the comfort of their home. Doe's interview, although it would not contain an admission, would offer plenty of clues as to the truth of the victim's statements.

Whether the criminal mind wants to hear this or not, it is against human nature to lie. Although the words may say one thing, the manner on which they are delivered, the suspects body language, and the answers to simple questions will give an experienced investigator all they need to chip away at the lies and find the truth. In this investigation, the lead was one of the best. She would approach her line of questioning tactically as if she was playing chess and in many ways the principles are the same. The investigator must know the path they want to take in preparation for a question to ask several minutes later, and although it may not be a confession, they are acknowledging the truth behind the allegations.

The lead would begin by asking Doe about his family, his daughters, and how their relationship was. Doe would answer that he has an ideal family; his children were well behaved, excellent students, and they had a very good relationship. She would ask about his marriage and whether they were happy. Of course, Doe stated they were. Setting a mood of comfort in an interview is essential. If an investigator goes in hard demanding answers to the accusations directly, the suspect will shut down and any potential information may be lost for good—and with it the chance for successful prosecution. Once Doe is relaxed, the investigator begins to talk about the victim, his daughter. Again, there is nothing asked about the allegations but more of how her personality is; is she happy, is she social or withdrawn, does she like to do things that other teenagers do, and so forth. Doe happily answers these questions and refers to her as a perfect child. She would then ask whether he thought his daughter was a liar or would lie, and Doe would say no. At this point, the investigator begins to turn the interview and begins to remind Doe of how he described his daughter and if he could think of any reason she would lie about this. He would say he does not know and that she is a very truthful person. Although in some eyes, this answer may seem neither an indictment of guilt nor just nervousness, to a trained investigator, it can be a small admission and acknowledgment to the truth of the allegations. Coupled with body language and nonverbal clues, it gives an investigator insight as to where to take the line of questioning. In Doe's case, it would only lead to more inconsistencies in the world he described his family lived in and the one in which the victim came forward to describe.

During the course of the interview, Doe would show affirmative physical gestures while the investigator was asking him questions and describing the acts his daughter reported. This should not be lost on the interviewer. For example, when the investigator explains to Doe that his daughter's report was very believable and descriptive, he can be seen shaking his head yes and responded by asking, "Could it be someone else?" The investigator should not give into this response and she did not by simply redirecting it back to Doe by telling him his daughter was very specific in telling investigators it was him, to which he responded "yeah."

Although Doe would not come out and admit to what he was accused of, there are plenty of verbal and physical admissions during this interview. The important thing for investigators to remember is that an interview, a good interview, should not and will not be over quickly. Good investigators can spend hours interviewing a suspect to obtain a confession or enough analysis of a subject to know whether they have the right person. Patience and pace of questioning is one of the most important things to have in the interview room. The good cop–bad cop routines only work on TV and have little place in the real world of investigations.

At this point, a more thorough follow-up interview with the victim will be done. Most states require specialized training to speak to children regarding abuse. During this interview, it is done in a more controlled environment and a lot slower than the original interview in which a brief overview of the allegations was obtained. This is where the investigator can establish timelines, how many times the assaults occurred, the locations, the manner in which they were done, and an overall more descriptive picture of what happened during this abuse. This interview is more essential for prosecution and conviction rather than the interview at the initiation of the case.

After the information is gathered and there is a general consensus, investigators will usually meet with each other and superiors to document a course of action and whether or not any stone has been left unturned. When there is an abundance of information in a case such as this, at some point, something may be forgotten and with more eyes looking at the puzzle, the odds of anything being missed are reduced.

Analysis of the Electronic Evidence

Once the evidence is seized, it has to be transported to a secure evidence locker, or in the case of an electronic evidence, to a secure lab until it can be imaged and analyzed for relevance in the case. Given the number of storage devices found at Doe's residence, the organization is imperative. The lead digital forensic investigator in this case marks all original evidence and documents serial numbers on photocopied hard drives with a form that he developed to assist the organization. An example of the form is shown in Figure 7.1.

It is recommended that investigators remember how important an organization is, develop their own refined method, and use it every time to establish a routine that if challenged by defense attorneys can be pointed to as consistent and successful. The refined method should be based on a proven method or combination of methods. The refined method may be an exact duplicate of some other organization's method, but as the investigator gains experience, there will likely be enhancements that need to be made.

AGENCY NAME

In this box information can be recorded such as the make and models of the computers seized and what attributes the computers have.

<table>
<tr>
<td>Agency: ____________________

Case: ____________________

Date: ____________________

Investigator: ____________________</td>
<td>Notes:</td>
</tr>
<tr>
<td>Device: ____________________

Serial #: ____________________

Model: ____________________

Drive Make: ____________________

Drive Serial #: ____________________

Description: ____________________

Size: ____________________

Hash: ____________________

Blocker: ____________________

Software used for Analysis: ____________________</td>
<td>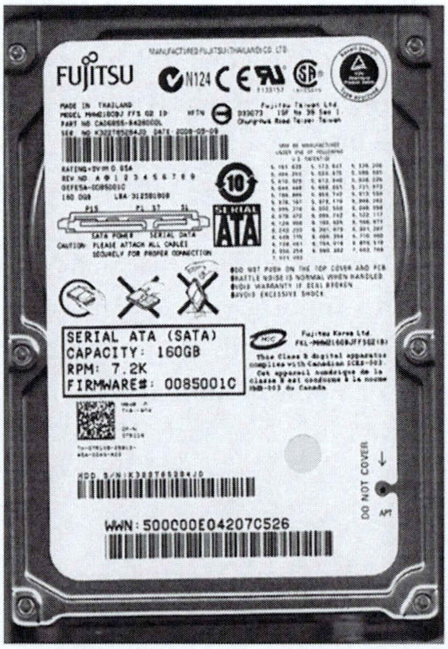</td>
</tr>
</table>

Figure 7.1 Hard drive acquisition form. Photocopy image of the suspect hard drive in order to document serial numbers.

For analyzing the evidence, there are many tools. For this case, we will focus on the major tools used. After imaging the evidence, AccessData's FTK software was used to analyze the image to search the evidence of the crime and child pornography that Doe showed is daughter. Katana's Lantern software was used to analyze Doe's iPhone and Mac computers. Again, there are other tools, but these are what were used in this case.

Prior to examinations, a bit for bit image must be taken from the suspect's original digital storage device, and verified with a digital fingerprint known as a hash. This is done on every hard drive examined in this case. During the examinations, the information provided by the interviews and what was listed in the search warrants indicated that there would be images of child sexual acts on Doe's computers. Keeping that in mind, it is important that it is the only thing that investigators search for. Otherwise, it has to be stated in the search warrant and probable cause has to be established to search other files.

The examination began by carving all image files from the storage devices. There were 90,000 at this point, and the examiner must sift through all of these images to find those that may depict the victim or other forms of child pornography. In this case, 500 images were located, which depicted child pornography, ranging from children posing nude to children performing intercourse with adult males. Further examination of storage devices would produce images of the victim nude in the shower, which were taken with Doe's iPhone. The digital examiner would then examine the picture data to verify they were taken with the suspect's iPhone, establish the victim's identity by showing the pictures to her mother, and prove the location of where the photo was taken by using the latitude and longitude information from the photo and plugging them into Google Earth, which showed the location of the family's home. The purpose of the examination and the forensic report is to not only tell the prosecutor and other investigators what was found, but to do it soundly and correctly so that it cannot be defeated in court. If the evidence in a case is altered or not stored and organized as pertains to the rules of evidence, the case will most likely not be successfully prosecuted.

As with the interview phase of the investigation, the analysis of digital media must be done with patience and care to produce the most thorough report of evidentiary value to the prosecutor and lead investigator in the case. Anything less than this is an injustice to the victims of the case, the officers involved, the prosecutor, and the community.

Prosecution and Testimony

After the evidence is submitted to the prosecutor, the case will go through the court process and procedures. I asked the prosecutor in this case what sort of things she looks at when she decides a strategy for trials like this. Her main concern in a case like this rested in the testimony of a child victim against her father, and that the testimony of digital forensic investigators did not go over the heads of the jurors. The examination of electronic evidence being a relatively new science may not only sound Greek to the average persons, but they may also lose interest and drift off into their own worlds and problems that are waiting for them outside the jury box. If that happens, it does not matter what happened prior to that in the case; they may miss an important point and that could be all the defense needs to raise the reasonable doubt for an acquittal.

Fortunately, in this case, the prosecutor stated that the victim in this case was strong and understood what needed to be done. She had the support of her mother and sister and her testimony would not be a concern. There were meetings with the prosecutor prior to the trial where reports are gone over several times and testimony is prepped and all the evidence needed is prepared and turned over to the prosecutor to be used for trial. Those of us in the forensic field believe that what we talk about most people will understand when it comes to the inner-workings of the computer and where the electronic evidence is stored. However, this is not the case. The lead investigator decided he would make a PowerPoint presentation to briefly explain to the jury where the evidence comes from and the definitions of some of the terms he would be using to explain his evidence. According to the prosecutor, this was a great idea and served the case well. The jurors seemed to understand and pay more attention after learning more about what the electronic evidence meant prior to hearing it asked in question form.

When testifying, it is also important to know to whom you are talking. The lawyers are asking the questions, but a witness is not trying to convince them but attempting to convince the jury. I have seen officers who have testified and never looked at the jury once. If you cannot address the jury and explain to them what you are trying to say, how are they supposed to make an informed decision on the guilt or innocence of the person on trial? Remembering to listen intently to the question and turning your body to address the entire jury and not just one person makes them feel involved in the proceeding and better understand what you are saying, rather than drifting off.

In this case, with all the electronic evidence, it is important to speak slowly and plainly to the jury. Yes, the PowerPoint helped to establish some knowledge, but the more calmly and simply you rely on the information, the more it will sink in. The defense attorney's job is to raise reasonable doubt in the investigators case, and they will do anything to do so. Doe's attorney would rely on trying to confuse the jury by undoing the plain descriptions of how the electronic evidence was found with technical terms and "what ifs," even going as far as to challenge the manner that websites redirect someone after clicking on a thumb nail. It is not the defense attorney's job to understand the technical aspects of the digital forensic field. Rather, it is to know enough to challenge the investigators answers, methods of evidence gathering and analysis, and raise enough doubt in the jury's mind to find their client not guilty.

Things to Consider

I have provided an outline of how this investigation occurred from the beginning to end, and some of the things that were considered and took place. Overall, most investigations can take place in the same general way provided a system is in place, and there is a standard that the investigator adheres to each and every time. Preparing your equipment and making certain that you have everything you need each and every time you arrive to a scene could and most likely will save you a lot of time in the long run. It will not only save you time, but also show others around you that you have a professional and disciplined mind set. Once the equipment is prepped and it is time to deploy to the scene, there are many factors to consider. In this case, there was a minimal risk of violence expected. That does not mean, however, that the investigators let their guard down. What it means is that they deployed to the scene with one uniformed officer and approached in a calm manner. If there are any indications in other investigations that you may be dealing with a person who has told friends and family that he or she will do anything to avoid prison or being caught, to kill police or himself or herself, a different approach has to be taken. In these situations, safety along with the preservation of evidence must be a priority, therefore, the approach and the manner in which the entry is made will be faster and more tactical. These approaches may include the use of an emergency response team or more uniformed officers. The time of day is also a consideration. If your intelligence suggests that the individual is up all night and sleeps all day, entry may need to wait until they are asleep or vice versa. Time will dictate how much information you can gather and how to prepare. If the investigator is given more time, more preparation and coordination can take place.

The manner in which your equipment and evidence is transported is also a detail that may often be overlooked. In many cases, your equipment costs thousands of dollars. Going cheap on cases and how you secure it may cost more in the long run. Hard cases that can be secured and stacked neatly in your vehicle will prevent damage. This is also the case with the evidence. Once the evidence is photographed, logged, and taken from the scene, there is no excuse for it to be damaged in transport. Your evidence and how you treat it can take your case from being a winner or a gamble on whether the suspect goes to jail for his or her crime or walk free. It can be as simple as mounting wooden boxes or crates to the floor of your evidence vehicle for purchasing extra hard cases for the evidence. The investigator should always have the proper bags and gloves to handle what is seized. Once the evidence is transported back to the facility, take care and caution to properly identify and tag each piece of the evidence before securing it in its proper locker or lab. The evidence is the key to your case, and there is no point in allowing yourself to become lazy at this point in the investigation. A misstep here can cause a dismissal on the case purely based on a technicality and damage your reputation as an investigator. This care should be taken throughout the process, analyzing, legal proceedings, and sentencing. When the case is being tried, the investigator may have to sign the evidence out and take it to court. The same rules apply and even more care should be considered, due to the multiple hands of the attorneys and in some cases jurors handling it.

In the time from seizure to sentencing, which can vary on a case by case basis, the evidentiary chain of custody must always be maintained. Some cases can drag on for months depending on motions made by the attorneys and some may be done within a 45 day window, but the chain must be kept from breaking. If one break occurs, that piece of evidence may become inadmissible and will probably destroy the case.

When the case is over and during the appeals process, the evidence is kept in the same manner until the appeal is heard and ruled on, at which time it can be destroyed or sold depending on the seizure orders of the agency. In all, take care of your equipment, your evidence, and how you maintain your secure facility. It will reflect not only on you or your investigation, but your agency and the investigations that are conducted.

Conclusion

From the origination of a complaint, through the fact finding, evidence gathering, testifying, and prosecution, whether or not the investigator is successful completely depends on that investigator. If an investigator cuts corners, does not show careful due diligence when conducting the investigation, or simply does not follow the rules of evidence, the results can be disastrous. Patience and showing a willingness to listen as well as pay attention to details will lead to success.

In Doe's investigation and eventual successful prosecution for the sexual assault of his daughter and possession of child pornography, the investigators I observed in my opinion were the picture of excellence within their organization, exhibiting patience and knowledge while conducting the investigation. They left no stone unturned, and showed they not only cared for doing the best job possible, but justice for the victim and her family as well. If anything is to be taken from this chapter, it should be that patience and the willingness to learn from observation, which will make you a better investigator.

After Doe was found guilty and sentenced to 25 years in prison, his other child came forward and was able to begin the healing process by admitting to authorities that Doe had sexually assaulted her as well. Doe was a child sexual predator, who not only pursued child pornography on the Internet, but preyed on his own children. Thanks to the investigators in this case, he can no longer do that and a family can attempt to move on.

8

REPORT WRITING AND PRESENTATION

Introduction

Report writing and presenting the findings are arts unto themselves. An investigator learns a lot about the subjects of the investigation, as well as what has occurred. However, much of what has been learned will be lost if the information is not put in the report. Putting information in investigation notes can be used to explain what is in the report and how it was arrived at, as well as background information about the investigation. The balance that an investigator has to grapple with is how much information to put in a report. Too much information and the details tend to be overlooked. If there are too little information, the report appears incomplete.

Many forensic tools generate reports from bookmarks and notes that an investigator made when working the case. Often there are options for the types of formats to generate, such as rtf, pdf, a hyperlinked document, or a web page. The problem is that the reports do not make room for information from other tools or sources. My preference is to generate an rtf or similar format report, import it into a tool such as Microsoft Word, and "make it pretty." Some forensic tools do not generate reports that are easily imported or modified in Word. An example would be the reports generated from Cellebrite.

Report Content and Considerations

At a minimum, reports should contain a title page, table of contents, engagement letter/reason for the investigation, investigator signature page, abstract/summary overview, examiner comments, and evidence. Most of the forensic reports do not provide a feature set that lets an investigator generate this type of report, which is why it is often necessary to import the various artifacts that need to be included in the report into one location.

A title page should include a title, the name of the case, and the case or court file number. Additionally, information about who prepared the report should also be part of the title page. This would include the investigator's name and title, agency/organization, any licenses, certifications or other qualifying information describing the investigator, and the date the report was created. In an increasing number of states, licensure as a professional investigator or law enforcement officer is required to conduct digital forensic investigations. Performing investigations without this credential is a felony.

The table of contents would provide location information for all sections and subsections in the report. For a summary report or a case brief, a table of contents may not be necessary. A good rule of thumb is to start using a table of contents when the report approaches 10 pages in length.

In a civil case or some other manner where an investigation is requested, I always ask for an engagement letter that includes authorization to conduct the investigation and an outline of what is being requested. This may vary for a criminal case, where a search warrant may be included. Since I am a professional investigator and not a law enforcement officer, I ask for written "request for assistance" when contacted by law enforcement to help and generally include that in place of the engagement letter in the report.

Most of the reports are read by a nontechnical audience, and that needs to be kept in mind by the person preparing the report. An abstract is likely necessary for a long report. The investigators comments are where the report will shine or fall flat. First of all, only facts should be reported, and if an investigator found something potentially pertinent to the case, it needs to be recorded. Similarly, if an investigator looked for something and did not locate it, that is a finding and it should be recorded. The spirit of what I mean by this is that not finding something may completely change the perception of guilt or innocence of someone. Failure to report the inability to find something can bias a report, and a biased report can be unethical and does not serve the cause of justice.

The point about the audience for reports being nontechnical may need to be addressed as part of the reporting process. Sometimes, a glossary of terms and/or a short technical primer on certain aspects of computer technology is in order so that a report can be properly understood. Glossaries are often included in a report, whereas technical primers are often separate documents or take the form of a verbal briefing prior to report presentation. The tool set that the investigator used should also be documented. As a side note, the investigator should be trained and experienced in the use of the tools used. Since tools change frequently, it is not practical to expect the examiner to be trained in all versions and tools used as long as the tools are a logical progression of previous training and experience. Think of this like going to a dentist. You expect the doctor to be trained and competent, but you do not expect them to have to go to a class each time they get a new drill bit. The reason why I bring this up is that I am aware of law enforcement agencies that are conducting digital forensic examinations where the investigator has little or no training in digital forensics, and in some cases, no formal education in computer technology.

The findings of an examination should be summarized in the examiner's comment section of the report. When conducting keyword searches during the investigation process, there may be thousands of hits. The examiner usually sort through the hits and bookmarks representative samples for inclusion in the report. The number of bookmarks can be in hundreds or thousands, which can make a report very lengthy. Without a technical background, most people get lost in the detail. The bookmarks and evidence should be logically arranged within the report and broken into sections. Sections might be things such as computer configuration information, e-mail, graphics, search engine searches conducted on the suspect computer, and so forth. There should be a short overview of each section within the examiner's comment portion of the report, followed by a reference to the first item of interest in each section. This may be a page number and/or a hyperlink within the document.

The evidence is what was found on the devices that were part of the investigation. As just mentioned, this should be logically sequenced and arranged by categories. This often starts with information documenting the devices, such as serial numbers, configuration information, and pictures of the devices. The pictures may be of the device where it was seized—with several angles so that cable connections and state information are documented. A drawing of the location may also be included, as well as a summary of the seizure process. Make sure to highlight that the source and image hashes match, and also that the hash of the image was taken at the conclusion of the report and that it also matches. The method used to find the evidence (i.e., sector math) and where it was located may also need to be included if it is pertinent to the case. For example, files that are hidden in an Alternate Data Stream, utilized encryption, packers, or have had their extensions modified can show intent, whereas finding a file in unallocated space could have an entirely different connotation and interpretation.

Some examiners feel that conclusions should also be included in the report. I am a bit on the fence on this one, and part of it is semantics. I will outline a few of the issues and you can draw your own "conclusion." It is paramount that reports should not include bias or conjecture. Drawing conclusions can interject both. The examiner's job is to find facts and it is up to the defense to explain how and why things could be found during the investigation. Juxtaposed to this, conclusions can simply be that user-id ABC downloaded file DEF from www.website.com on a certain date. Conclusions can also be that 5000 illegal images were found on the computer. However, placing Bad Guy at the keyboard using userid ABC at the time in question can be difficult. Things that can aid this cause are finding logins to things like Bad Guy's Facebook and e-mail accounts at a similar time, and even better, finding things like Facebook postings and e-mail messages created using Bad Guy's account. A defense attorney only needs to explain one conclusion to begin to enter the realm of reasonable doubt, so be very careful with conclusions.

Sample Reports

A few sample reports follow including a summary report for a computer forensic exam, a mobile device report from Katana's Lantern, and a portion of a cell examination from Cellebrite. Before we review the reports, I would like to point out that the method of distribution should be considered. The examiner should check with the prosecutor and/ or judge regarding guidelines for reports that include child pornography, as copying the images found on the devices into the report may technically be interpreted as distribution. Again, ask that the guidelines be in writing. Another consideration is the medium or manner in which the reports are distributed. I am not a fan of e-mail distribution for a variety of reasons including report tampering and unauthorized access.

It is not too difficult to forward a report. It also may be a security issue. My preference is usually a write-once medium such as a DVD or CD-ROM. Spend an extra 50 cents and use a LightScribe® disk rather than writing on the disk with a Sharpie or using a sticker label. This is your first chance to make an impression about your report, and you can only make one first impression. The second impression is important too—make sure that it is organized similar to the way previously described. I have had attorneys send me reports from "the opposing side" to interpret because the examiner simply used the report generation features in the forensic tools and did not take the time to organize and explain the findings within the body of the report.

I include a ReadMe.txt file on the DVD with the report. Sample test from the ReadMe:

> The media contained on this disk is solely intended for Pleasantville County Court File No. 13-2399-DD. Those not authorized as part of this case should not review this disk. Please return to Mirean Law Office, Plankton, MI 49444.

Following is a sample computer forensics report. Please realize that in the interest of space that I attempted to make this report short and many of the artifacts are only partial representations. With this in mind, some exhibit representations are in plain text rather than rebuilt web pages.

COMPUTER FORENSICS REPORT

Badguy vs. Badguy

Court File No. 13-65765-MM

Prepared by Dr. Greg Gogolin
Michigan Digital Forensics, LLC
PI License # 1231-233209
CISSP, EnCE, PMP
August 27, 2013

Copy of signature page goes here. I usually sign a statement and scan it in here.
  Copy of commission/authorization to perform investigation goes here. Same thing—I scan it in.

Case 13-65765-MM Badguy
Preliminary Report
Submitted by Dr. Greg Gogolin
8/27/13

An examination was conducted in August 2013, of the Hewlett Packard Desktop Tower dc6000MT DZ446A4 2UB198041R running Windows XP sp3 build.08513-211 with an accurate BIOS time/date configuration. Further, technical characteristics are listed subsequently in the Administrative Information portion of this report. This investigation was conducted using EnCase Forensic version 6.18 with a Tableau T35es write blocker with serial number TB352322. The MD5 hash of the original drive was 004fsbf5fe806f-41ca4ef4e556a8a8e9. The MD5 hash of the acquisition/image was 004fsbf5fe-806f41ca4ef4e556a8a8e9. The MD5 hash at the conclusion of the investigation was 004fsbf5fe806f41ca4ef4e556a8a8e9.

The computer contains hundreds of pictures of family vacations, fishing trips, and other activities, as well as software consistent with family computer use. Several e-mail documents were recovered upon performing keyword searches on e-mail addresses. There were several documents from Real Badguy to Sweet Stuff detailing an ongoing affair during June and July 2007 beginning on page 4 of this report—item #36. Page 6 beginning with item #42 describes exchange of untraceable cell phones between unknown parties. There are also e-mail exchanges between Real Badguy and Back Stabber in 2005 detailing porn preferences (preference for young) and exchanging pornographic material on page 6—item #38. These e-mails led to the initial discovery of hundreds of pornographic images and 42 pornographic movie files.

The pornographic movies and a large number of pornographic images were resident on the computer in an undeleted state. Anyone who was at the computer could have viewed these images. Among these undeleted photographs were pictures of Real Badguy wearing a Tutu and no underwear, with four of the photographs displaying his genitals. The theme in the movies tended to be young girls. Stamped into the media of some of the videos were logos of ExploitedTeens.com, ExploitedBabySitters.com, TeenxxxHardCore.com, and ExploitedCollegeGirls.com. Some of the videos portrayed a school setting between a male teacher and a female student. The female characteristics sometimes included dressing in tube socks and tennis shoes, pig tails, and other things consistent with young girls.

More troubling was the discovery of 332 anime images of naked young girls. Many had the facial and body features consistent with girls in elementary or perhaps middle school. Several had young facial characteristics and fully developed bodies. At this point I stopped investigating and contacted law enforcement for guidance. Upon discussion with the Michigan State Police Internet Crimes Against Children (ICAC) Digital Crime Unit, it was determined that the hard drive should be turned over to them for review. The drive was examined by ICAC and it was determined that the images were not able to be confirmed as child pornography. With this August 26, 2013 finding, the investigation was resumed.

Upon reconstruction of pictures from unallocated disk space, an additional 13,645 graphic files were recovered. Thousands of these images were pornographic, including 34 more naked anime images. Others were young girls about to engage in sexual intercourse or in various stages of undress.

Additional pornographic images that were recovered included a variety of sexual situations including intercourse, fellatio, anal, multiple penetration, lesbian, gay, S & M, obese people, young females, as well as other situations. Because of the large volume of pornographic images, time did not allow for accurate counting of the various types of images of each category. Some of the young female pictures appear to be nearly as young in appearance as those depicted in the anime.

Additional findings include significant activity on social networking, gaming, fantasy, and virtual world web sites. Web sites included Facebook, YoVille, FarmVille, addicting games, tinier me, FrontierVille, Garden Life, and a variety of other sites. Temporary folders indicate activity with AddictingGames.com, AmateurGalore.net, EveryThinGirl.com, DirectSex.com, XMissy.nl, MySex Games.com, SexGamesFree.net, AdultSwim.com, PornHub.com, PronMinded. com, PornoTube.com, PornHost.tv, RedTube.com, 2AdultFlashGames.com, SkinVideo.com, Thrixxx.com, XMissyPorn.com, and MegaPorn.com. There are many dozen other legitimate temporary folders.

In summary, this computer has an unusually large and diverse collection of pornographic files and images consistent with an exorbitant affinity toward pornography.

On August 17, 2013, the company computers used by Real and Nota Badguy were imaged and a preliminary review has been conducted. Real's computer is CT 9842202H1AGKH8, 6E388C0711553, E1VCLBZEL4399, with Maxtor hard drive P/N 244132-065. Asset tag is V88Y6-9DVVV-DNNXC-DVXDT-XX2ZZ, 00035-518-117-104. Nota's computer is CT 268860sH1QZJM9, BE 356L0711233, E1UD5F3BB4499. Asset tag is FXXQW-5GCCH-VBVY9-J6XJJ-XXYQG, 00235-518-667-002. The summary reports for these computers are separate from this report.

Two video files were on Real's computer that appear to be self-produced by Real on Wednesday, September 2, 2009. The intended recipient is referred to as "babe," which is the name used to address Sweet Stuff in the 2007 e-mails. He mentions that he loves the recipient and hopes to catch that person online that day. The computer does not have a lot of pornography on it, but it does have two naked images of Manessa Nudgins. There was question about whether these images were child pornography when they first surface on the Internet.

Also on the computer are a large number of family pictures similar to the previously described HP Tower home computer. Temporary folders indicate activity with AddictingGames.com, AmateurGalore.net, SexGamesFree. net, AdultSwim.com, PornHub.com, PornoTube.com, RedTube.com, and MegaPorn.com. There are many dozen other legitimate temporary folders.

The examination of these computers is not yet complete.

Administrative Information (HP Tower)

Volume

File System	NTFS	Drive Type	Fixed
Sectors per Cluster	8	Bytes per Sector	512
Total Sectors	156,280,257	Total Capacity	80,015,491,072 Bytes (74.5 GB)
Total Clusters	19,535,032	Unallocated	16,783,519,744 Bytes (15.6 GB)
Free Clusters	4,097,539	Allocated	63,231,971,328 Bytes (58.9 GB)
Volume Name		Volume Offset	63
Id	S-1-5-21-836200215- 621444749-2340013444		
Serial Number	50DD-UU7B		
Full Serial Number	26A2E72950XXVX7B		
Driver Information	NTFS 3.1		

Device

Name	Seagate AT830022S
Actual Date	07/27/10 09:34:59PM
Target Date	07/27/10 09:34:59PM
File Path	G:\Miraen\Seagate\Seagate AT830022S.E01
Case Number	Miraen
Evidence Number	Seagate AT830022S
Examiner Name	Greg Gogolin, Ph.D.
Notes	Miraen—HP—80 gig hdd tower
Serial Number	Ø
Drive Type	Fixed
File Integrity	Completely Verified, 0 Errors
Acquisition Hash	004fsbf5fe806f41ca4ef4e556a8a8e9
Verify Hash	004fsbf5fe806f41ca4ef4e556a8a8e9
GUID	2110b2725d7751408f21b74739efcd33
EnCase Version	6.11
System Version	Windows XP
Fastbloced	No
Neutrino	No
Is Physical	Yes
Raid RHS	No

(Continued)

Raid Stripe Size	0
Error Granularity	64
Process Id	0
Index File	G:\Miraen\Index\Seagate AT830022S- 2270b2725d651408f21b74739efcd33.Index
Acquisition Info	No
Sources	No
Subjects	No
Read Errors	0
Missing Sectors	0
Disk Elements	No
CRC Errors	0
Compression	Good
Total Size	80,026,361,856 Bytes (74.5GB)
Total Sectors	156,301,488
Disk Signature	449C879C

Partitions

Code	Type	Start Sector	Total Sectors	Size
07	NTFS	0	156,280,320	74.5 GB
00	Recovered	156,280,256	156,280,319	74.5 GB

Figure 8.1 shows the service tag identifying HP Tower computer (product key and serial numbers obscured for security purposes).

Figure 8.2 depicts the back of the HP Tower computer as received July 26, 2013.

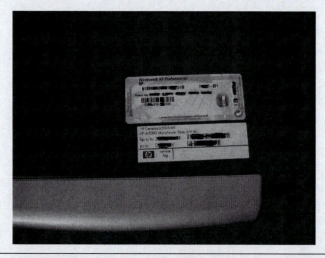

Figure 8.1   Picture of service tag.

Figure 8.2   Picture of back of HP Tower.

E-MAIL

36) Miraen\Seagate AT830022S\C\Documents and Settings\Administrator\
Application Data\Mozilla\Profiles\Real\v9jud8ae.slt\Mail\Local Folders\Trash

Letters of Interest

```
From - Thu Jul 12 11:06:25 2007
X-Mozilla-Status: 0019
X-Mozilla-Status2: 00800000
Message-ID: <4194436B.4040704@thebasementco.com>
```
Date: Thu, 12 Jul 2007 11:06:19 -0400
From: Real Badguy <Real@thebasementco.com>
```
User-Agent: Mozilla/5.0 (Windows; U; Windows NT 5.1; en-US; rv:1.7.2)
Gecko/20040804 Netscape/7.
2 (ax)
X-Accept-Language: en-us, en
MIME-Version: 1.0
```
To: Sweet Stuff <Sweet@thebasementco.com>
```
Subject: Re: Hey…
References: <469633AC.1140507@thebasementco.com>
          <46964B3B.1170500@thebasementco.com>
In-Reply-To: <46964B3B.1170500@thebasementco.com>
Content-Type: text/plain; charset = ISO-8859-1; format = flowed
Content-Transfer-Encoding: 7bit
So how was Johny last night?
And what about your sister? How was she doing?
Yeah, this is only the beginning of us, and the end of the others
The beautiful thing is that, we will never be apart from each other.
So let's get rid of the others from our lives.
~ Real
Sweet Stuff wrote:
> Real Badguy wrote:
>
>> Just filled up with gas and thought of you.
>>
```

```
>> I didn't want to leave this morning but had to let the cat out.
>>
>> I miss you already…
>>
>> ~ Real
>>
>>
>>
>>
From - Thu Jul 12 11:13:32 2007
X-Mozilla-Status: 0019
X-Mozilla-Status2: 00800000
Message-ID: <4696551B.5080001@thebasementco.com>
```

Date: Thu, 12 Jul 2007 11:13:31 -0400
From: Real Badguy <Real@thebasementco.com>

```
User-Agent: Mozilla/5.0 (Windows; U; Windows NT 5.1; en-US; rv:1.7.2)
Gecko/20040804 Netscape/7.
2 (ax)
X-Accept-Language: en-us, en
MIME-Version: 1.0
```

To: Sweet Stuff <Sweet@thebasementco.com>

```
Subject: Re: Hey Sweetie
References: <469993AC.9040507@thebasementco.com>
            <46999B3B.6070500@thebasementco.com>
In-Reply-To: <46999B3B.6070500@thebasementco.com>
Content-Type: text/plain; charset = us-ascii; format = flowed
Content-Transfer-Encoding: 7bit
> how funny people can be so special isn't it!:)
> i was thinking about getting together.
>
> well i just got off the phone with johny. Not good.
> well my grandmother just called.
> yeah the thing about this is just the start.
If you just need me to hold you so you can let it all out, let me do
that to you…I love to manipulate people…~ Real
>
>
>
>
>
>
```

How to Hook Up at Hotels

```
From - Thu Jun 28 10:23:41 2007
X-Mozilla-Status: 0009
X-Mozilla-Status2: 00800000
Message-ID: <4683C466.30200@thebasementco.com>
```

Date: Thu, 28 Jun 2007 10:23:34 -0400
From: Real Badguy <Real@thebasementco.com>

```
User-Agent: Mozilla/5.0 (Windows; U; Windows NT 5.1; en-US; rv:1.7.2)
Gecko/20040804 Netscape/7.
2 (ax)
X-Accept-Language: en-us, en
MIME-Version: 1.0
```
To: Sweet Stuff <Sweet@thebasementco.com>
Subject: 1st Shift:-(
```
Content-Type: text/plain; charset = ISO-8859-1; format = flowed
Content-Transfer-Encoding: 7bit
The FairCreek Inn is down by the Summer Inn Express and the Modest Inn
by the mall in Hookup City. Should be nice.
```

38) Miraen\Seagate AT830022S\C\Documents and Settings\Administrator\ Application Data\Mozilla\Profiles\Real\v9juda9e.slt\Mail\mail.mybasementcompany .com\Sent

Porn Preferences

```
From - Mon Jul 11 00:25:28 2005
X-Mozilla-Status: 0001
X-Mozilla-Status2: 00800000
Message-ID: <42D1F4B2.5540807@mybasementcompany.com>
```
Date: Mon, 11 Jul 2005 00:25:22 -0400
From: Real Badguy <Real@mybasementcompany.com>
```
User-Agent: Mozilla/5.0 (Windows; U; Windows NT 5.1; en-US; rv:1.7.2)
Gecko/21140804 Netscape/7.
2 (ax)
X-Accept-Language: en-us, en
MIME-Version: 1.0
```
To: That Back Stabber <backstabber@earthlink.net>
Subject: Itsy bitsy teeny weeny…
```
Did you look in the movie setup? There should be a Subtitles option.
>
>I was hoping that all the actors were live
> and just the background digital. If I wanted all digital I could
> watch Fantastic Fantasy: The demons within. I played FF from the
> very beginning and don't remember any of the stuff from the movie
> *L* But it is a pretty cool flick.
FF kinda intrigued me early on but I never watched it. It didn't seem
to have much in the plot.
>
> Depends. I'm pretty picky about porn. I like ….
>
```

Untraceable Cell Phones

42) Miraen\Seagate AT830022S\C\Documents and Settings\Administrator\ Local Settings\Temp\WER74a8.dir11\firefox.exe.hdmp request for untraceable cell phones

Does anyone have untraceable cell phones to sell me?

43) Miraen\Seagate AT830022S\C\Documents and Settings\Administrator\Local Settings\Temp\WER74a8.dir11\firefox.exe.hdmp

I need Untraceable Cell Phones

While a report can be much longer, this should be enough to give you a general feel for a report. In a situation where there are video and audio files, my preference is to create a directory on the DVD and export the files to that directory. I would then reference the directory containing the video and audio files in the examiner comments section.

The following is a sample cover letter that I often use to accompany a mobile report.

MICHIGAN DIGITAL FORENSICS, LLC

555 Main
Traverse City, MI 49684
www.MichiganDigitalForensics.com

February 14, 2014

Gosner Goodner
101 North Main Street
Johansville, IL 62625

RE: Verizon LGVN250—Data Retrieval

Mr. Goodner:

There are three types of extracts that I was able to perform on the Verizon LGVN250 CDMA MIN 6183382628 S/N 00D5YSF2332416 that are stored on the enclosed DVD:

1) **Logical Extraction**—found in LG CDMA VN-250 Cosmos Logical Extraction folder (view report.html)
2) **File System Extraction**—found in LG CDMA VN-250 Cosmos File System Extraction folder (view report.pdf)
3) **Physical Extraction**—found in LG CDMA VN-250 Cosmos Physical Extraction folder (view report.pdf)

Specific to the graphics and text messages sought:

There were several addresses, phone numbers, text messages, and images recovered in the time frame in question, primarily viewable in the File System Extraction and Physical Extraction reports. Both these reports include recovered deleted files and artifacts.

Greg Gogolin, Ph.D.
CISSP, EnCE, PI

The last sample report that we will review was generated from Katana's Lantern doing an acquisition of my iPad. Much of the information has been deleted for security purposes, but it gives you an idea of what a generated report would look like. Figure 8.3 is a screenshot of the Lantern interface, followed by the report.

Figure 8.4 is the beginning of a Lantern report. Some of the information have been obscured for security purposes. The Evidence Summary section contains hyperlinks to the corresponding artifacts. For example, clicking on the Notes hyperlink will go to the four notes that were extracted from the iPad. The Camera hyperlink will go to the seven pictures on the iPad.

The way many reports are presented, including the report in Figure 8.4, is as a scrollable document. In case you did not notice, I find Opera to be the best browser to view these reports, in part because of the zoom in/out feature that is built into the browser. It is possible to get plug-ins or other techniques to perform this in other browsers, but it is not as elegant as Opera.

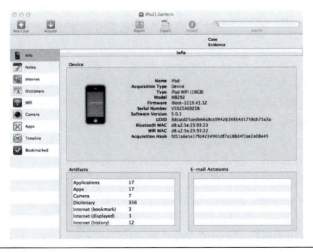

Figure 8.3   Katana's Lantern.

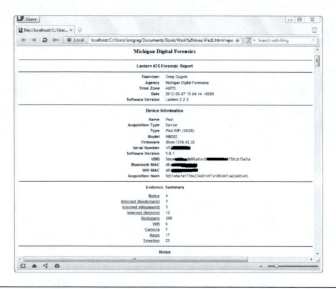

Figure 8.4   iPad report generated by Lantern.

Presenting and Testifying

There are a few basic things to remember when presenting findings, whether it is in a corporate meeting, deposition, or court situation. The first is to stick to the facts and present what you know. Be very careful when asked for conjecture or opinions. Lawyers tend to try to summarize things and ask you if it is an accurate statement and/or something you agree with. It usually is better to use your own words because a lawyer likely has something in mind when they ask you something, and they may be leading you around a corner where you do not want to go to. Before you know it, you are in a place that can be difficult to work out of, and your work may be discredited. Trust no one may be a bit harsh, but it may be the best place to start.

Laws regarding depositions vary, so it is important to gain an understanding of the environment prior to providing a deposition. It is a legal record, so accuracy is critical. Some states allow you to review the deposition transcription to make sure that it is accurately recorded. The time frame that is allowable for this review—and when you can request a review—are points that you want to be clear on prior to the deposition. Consider stating at the beginning of the deposition that you would like to review it before it is submitted. I reviewed one of my own depositions and found that I was attributed a comment that was actually stated by the opposing counsel. It was lucky that I found this in the review because the statement would have completely changed the character of my testimony had the inaccurate attribution not been corrected.

Depositions can be taken at just about any location. I have been deposed in places such as a library and a law office. During the deposition, it is good practice to ask for clarification of any question that you do not understand or that appears ambiguous. Make sure that you are comfortable. Do not be afraid to ask for breaks or other comfort measures, especially if it will be a lengthy process. It is okay to bring and take notes, and there may be other people as witnesses. There will also be a court reporter recording the proceedings.

Depositions record what was stated, but they are not useful in understanding how something was stated or body language. However, body language and how things were stated are important in court proceedings or corporate settings. Eye contact, confident posture, and a good appearance are important factors. Unspoken factors can be the most important aspect of your testimony.

Archiving

A case is ready to be archived once it has been presented. The case files, images, reports, correspondence, and other documentation all need to be part of this process. An examiner may make some final notes to help serve as a memory refresh or simply conclude the documentation process. A piece that is often overlooked is that the tools that are used for the case need to be archived as well. It is not a good situation if you need to review a case from a couple of years ago and are unable to bring it up or replicate results in the current version of the tools. That alone may lay groundwork for a successful appeal. My preference is to use an external USB hard drive for archiving. It is also a good idea to keep an old computer around for old cases as the new version of the operating system may not support the archived tool set. Eventually, some cases may reach a point where archived information can be deleted or destroyed. It is best to have a policy that has had legal review that governs when and if case information can be deleted or destroyed.

Summary

The information and reports that were presented are intended as a general guide to provide an idea about what digital forensic reports should include and how they are presented. Cases vary and so do the requirements of the report. The point of the chapter is that you need to make sure basic information is included to make a viable report, and above all, pay particular attention to accuracy and ethical practices—remember, people's lives depend on the outcome of our work.

9

SOCIAL MEDIA FORENSICS

DR. BARBARA L. CIARAMITARO

Introduction to Social Media

With the advent of Web 2.0 and the introduction of user-created content and collaboration came a set of Internet-based sites and tools that are collectively known as social media. Social media refers to Internet-based technology tools that allow individuals to communicate, collaborate, and establish a community with others. There are several categories of social media, each of which provides different information and functionality to its users. We will review the basic elements of the most common social media tools and sites.

Social Networking

Social networking sites such as Facebook (www.facebook.com) and Google+ (www.google+.com) provide users an environment where they can create personal profiles and post updates to notify "friends" about their current activities. It incorporates other social media tools such as messaging, e-mail, video chat, location identification, and the posting of multimedia content. Users can selectively add friends and send them messages or post comments on their wall. Facebook users can also join networks organized by city, workplace, school, region, or any other topic of interest.

E-Mail

Internet-based e-mail is the most highly used social media tool. Internet-based e-mail involves the sending and receiving of messages, attached documents, and multimedia content to and from users through the Internet. There are a plethora of Internet e-mail providers, but the most common and popular providers are Google and Microsoft.

Blogs

A blog (weblog) is a social media site maintained by an individual or organization with regular entries of commentaries or descriptions of events. Blog entries are commonly displayed in reverse chronological order. Many blogs provide commentary on a particular subject, whereas others function as more personal online diaries. A typical blog uses text, images, and links to other blogs, as well as websites and other media related to its topic. The ability of blog reviewers to leave comments is considered an important part of establishing interactivity and relationships through blogs. There are specific blog search engines such as Technorati (http://technorati.com) and Digg (http://digg.com) that allow users to conduct searches of blog postings.

Microblogs

Microblogging differs from blogs in that they allow users a very limited amount of text space to create postings. The most well-known microblogging tool is Twitter. Twitter (www.twitter.com) is a free microblogging service that allows its users to send and receive messages known as tweets. Tweets are text-based posts of up to 140 characters displayed on the author's profile page and delivered to the author's subscribers who are known as followers.

Event Coordination

The Internet can be used to plan meetings of users with shared interests. One event coordination social media tool is Meetup (www.meetup.com), which is an online portal that facilitates offline group meetings in various localities around the world. It allows members to find and join groups unified by a common interest, such as politics, books, games, movies, health, pets, careers, or hobbies.

Location Identification

A relatively recent addition to social media is the use of technology by providers such as Foursquare (www.foursqare.com), to utilize mobile device GPS coordinates to identify and record the location of a user at any specific time. These tools are referred to as location-based technologies. In many cases, this user-specific location information is then posted to one of the user's social networking sites such as Facebook.

Multimedia Sharing

The Internet has become a central repository for the sharing of user-created multimedia content such as photographs and videos. Flickr (www.flickr.com) is a popular social media site where users post their photographs. An interesting aspect of these types of photo sites is the ability to tag the photo with an identifier, making it easier for searches of particular types of photos. YouTube (www.youtube.com) is a social media site where user-generated videos are posted. A common characteristic of multimedia sharing sites is the ability for other users to rate or grade the interest or quality of the posting. This user rating system provides information to allow some content to spread very quickly in popularity.

Search

Searching the Internet for items of interest has become one of the most popular social media activities. In the United States, the most popular search engines include Google (www.google.com), Microsoft Bing (www.bing.com), and Yahoo! (www.yahoo.com). Other countries, however, have established their own specific search engines such as Baidu (www.baidu.com) in China. There are also many specialty search engines that can be used for focused searches for specific content. For example, Academic Index and Base are two academic search engines useful for formal academic research (Blog@bau, 2011). There are many other specialized search engines that focus on targeted media types such as multimedia content searches. Additionally, there are search engines that search for specific content in various domains such as robots, agriculture, and geospatial data (Anglia Ruskin University, 2010).

Wikis

A wiki is a website that is created to support the collaborative development of content by multiple users. The most common wiki is Wikipedia (www.wikipedia.com). Depending on the amount of access rights provided, users can add new content or modify the existing content. Wiki software keeps a record of each edit and editor, so that a wiki page can be restored to an earlier version in the event erroneous data are posted. Wikis are also identified by their ability to link content in one page to the content in one or more other pages.

Web Conferencing

Web conferencing is a technology tool used to connect participants in disparate locations to a central communication point. Web conferencing software can provide several functionalities including text chat, video conferencing, sharing of desktops, sharing of files, polling, and discussion sessions. Some web conferencing tools allow the sessions to be recorded and saved for future use.

Virtual Worlds

Virtual worlds are digital worlds. They are created using computer technologies. Virtual worlds often model elements of the real world such as buildings, roads, trees, and other environmental elements. Participants in virtual worlds use avatars to represent themselves. Avatars are graphic characters that can resemble humans, animals, or mythical creatures. Virtual worlds allow multiple users to share a common space that is represented in visual formats employing a variety of two- and three-dimensional designs. Immersion is an important aspect of virtual worlds. The more participants feel that they are a part of the digitally created world, the more they will interact and participate in the virtual world activities. Second Life is a well-known virtual world that provides its users the opportunity to create their environment. Additionally, sophisticate games such as World of Warcraft are also considered virtual worlds.

Social Media Forensics

The most common element of all the social media sites and technologies described earlier is the massive amount of information posted, created, and linked to by individual users. These data collections provide forensic investigators with an invaluable resource useful in a variety of investigations and analyses. Let us now examine the various social media tools with a focus on using them to conduct forensic investigations.

Forensic investigation involves looking for digital evidence and information in support of investigations conducted by the law enforcement personnel, military organizations, internal investigators, private investigators, and researchers. As you have learned so far in this chapter, forensic investigation involves two key elements: data and people. When we consider forensic investigation of social media, we also rely on these two elements. How can we track the flow of data and information through social media sites and technologies? How can we track people, their roles and place in an organizational structure, and their knowledge and information through social media?

There are some significant distinctions between traditional digital forensics and social media forensics that are important to highlight. In a traditional case of digital forensics, one or more computer devices are examined for evidence or relevant information. The focus is primarily on a single medium, the computer. In addition, in traditional digital forensics, the focus is often on a single individual or small group of individuals. In social media forensics, however, the focus is much broader. One or more persons of interest may post information in any number of social media sites, using any number of social media technologies. In addition, social media is often used to organize events, of which some may have nefarious or hostile intent. Social media forensic analysis, by its very nature, will also involve a degree of social network analysis in which organizational structures and key players are examined and identified. When conducting a social media forensic examination, it is important to be much broader in the search for evidence or relevant information. We will now look at some examples of social media investigations using social media forensics including street gangs, terrorist organizations, and white collar crimes.

Street Gangs

Street gangs are organized groups of individuals, often under the age of 21, who follow relatively strict rules of conduct. Gang membership may involve rites of passage that require them to prove their loyalty and bravado through crimes and attacks against other gangs (Walker, 2011). In many parts of the country, street gangs are considered the source of a significant amount of crime including drugs, prostitution, robberies, and assaults. The leaders of a street gang are usually very powerful and direct the activities of its members. There is often a wall of anonymity between themselves and the members performing the crimes. Identifying and neutralizing the leadership in a street gang can be a very effective form of crime control.

Street gangs often use various social media tools to communicate among their members and plan events. Two common social media tools are Facebook and Twitter (Watkins, 2010). Facebook is used to communicate with the entire gang often through the use of the Facebook Groups capability. The gang members may post photos, videos, or other information about their activities to gain approval or recognition. Gangs often use Twitter to send messages as to meeting location, crime locations, or other gang-related activities (Nurwisah, 2010). The gang members will often use pseudo names and special e-mail addresses when they use these social media tools. Lastly, the use of mobile technologies to access social media sites and tools are also commonly used.

The first step is to identify the potential social media sources of evidence and information for a gang investigation. These include Facebook, Twitter, location-based identification, multimedia photos and videos, e-mail, and mobile access. Each of these social media sources provides avenues for forensic investigation and analysis.

Facebook can provide various types of information to aid in the social media investigation (Nurwisah, 2010). The first goal of Facebook investigation is to try to achieve a view of posted information as a friend or group member. In the most optimum investigation, a law enforcement member is able to become accepted as Facebook "friend" and group member (Moilistina, 2011). Through the use of user profiles, the gang members can post various types of information that can lead to their individual identification such as references to activities or locations. Another Facebook friend or group member would be able to see this information.

However, even if "friendship" or group membership is not achieved by the investigator, there are two other forensic investigatory approaches. The first is to identify the username and password of one or more members of the gang. Second, the use of groups in Facebook provides an avenue for investigation and gang member identification. There are several techniques that can be used to obtain usernames and passwords to social media sites. One common approach is to establish a rogue wireless access point in a Wi-Fi location and capture the messages sent through that network. This could be a very effective approach to capturing the gang members' identification. A police officer could simply locate their laptop near a common Wi-Fi meeting point of the gang members, such as coffee houses or fast-food restaurants. As the gang members post their messages, their transmissions would be captured by the law enforcement personnel as approved in a legal warrant.

Another approach is to obtain the gang member's e-mail address and use that address to access the Facebook password through the "Forgot Password" function (Rafay Hacking Articles, 2010). A third approach is simply to uncover a password using the many password cracking tools that are available. Using any of these techniques, once the username and password combination is known, it is possible to closely track the messages posted by the associated gang members in Facebook to solve or preempt the occurrence of crimes.

The second approach to identifying the gang members through Facebook is through the use of Facebook Groups and designated websites. A 2010 study

(Wondracek, 2010) describes a technique to uncover the members of social networking groups as they visit designated website locations. Their study found that the information stored by social networking site about the group membership of a user was adequate to uniquely identify the members of the group visiting the website. The technique described uses "web browser history stealing attack" to accomplish this goal. As a result, when a social network user visits a designated website, the website can launch this "de-anonymization attack" and learn the identity of its visitors (Wondracek, 2010).

Gangs also use Twitter to communicate short messages quickly through their organization such as meeting or crime locations. Similar to Facebook, these Twitter accounts can lead to the identity of the gang members by uncovering their password and gaining access to their account. Password cracking techniques are very successful in uncovering Twitter passwords (Jeffries, 2011).

Both Twitter and Facebook are common mediums to share photographs by posting them in these social media sites. Many people do not realize that photographs taken by most mobile phones today store location, date, and time information about where the picture was taken as part of the metadata for the photograph. These metadata become available when the photo is posted to a social media site such as Facebook or Twitter. As a result, by examining the properties of the photo, the date, time, and longitude and latitude of its location can be determined (Ulbricht, 2011). The location, date, and time information are stored with the pictures as part of the Exchangeable Image File (EXIF) that is generally stored on both JPEG and TIFF images (Windows Guides, 2011). This information can prove to be very helpful to the law enforcement personnel, when they are investigating criminal activity by the gang members.

Terrorist Activity

> Terrorists have traditionally sought to exploit new and alternative media, particularly on the Internet, to spread their propaganda and to a lesser extent, operational and tactical guidance to prospective supporters.... As part of this trend, jihad supporters and mujahideen are increasingly using Facebook, one of the largest, most popular and diverse social networking sites, both in the United States and globally, to propagate operational information....
>
> **(Public Intelligence, 2010)**

An additional challenge posed by the terrorist organizations in their use of Facebook and other social media sites is the use of non-English languages such as Arabic, Urdu, Indonesian, and other less known languages (Public Intelligence, 2010).

Terrorist organizations are using social media sites such as Facebook and Twitter as a means to communicate with members and other organizations with shared goals (Public Intelligence, 2010; Washington Times, 2011). Estimates have found that 90% of current online terrorist activity occurs in social networking sites (Counter-Terrorism Implementation Task Force [CTITF], 2011). They use social media to share operational and tactical information such as recipes for bombs and maintenance of AK-47 weapons. Terrorist groups use social media to promote their message and encourage the spread of their missions to new members by linking to other extremist groups and sites. They also use social media for "remote reconnaissance for targeting purposes" (Public Intelligence, 2010). It is interesting that terrorist groups also commonly post messages on how to achieve anonymity within social media sites by using fictional data and new and unique passwords (Public Intelligence, 2010).

The use of social media sites by designated terrorist organizations is prohibited by law in the United States. However, the careful and anonymous use of social media sites by terrorists has made it difficult for investigators to isolate and assess credible terrorist threats through Facebook, due to its vast use by many terrorist organizations and the lack of verifiable user biographical information (Public Intelligence, 2010).

However, there is some current activity that is assisting in the investigation of terrorist use of social media. The University of Arizona is involved in a current research project referred to as the "Dark Web," which uses a variety of techniques to sort through the voluminous postings by the terrorist organizations on social media sites. They use these various posts to identify relationships and links between the various terrorist groups and activities (KVOA.Com, 2011). A similar project is currently being undertaken by Europol's "Check the Web" project (CTITF, 2011).

It is interesting to note that the terrorist organizations also use virtual worlds as a tool to organize and train (PR Newswire, 2011). Virtual worlds such as Second Life and World of Warcraft have become simulated training environments for the terrorist organizations using virtual representations of real weapons (CTITF, 2011). It is predicted that in addition to the continued use of virtual worlds for organization and training purposes, they will be used for fund-raising, terrorist finance, and money laundering (CTITF, 2011). A few years ago, IARPA issued a request for research proposals, referred to as the Reynard project. The focus of the request was for research on the ways to identify behavioral indicators in virtual worlds and multiuser online games that are related to the user's real-world characteristics with the goal of being able to automatically detect "suspicious behavior" in the virtual world (Mountjoy, 2008).

As the number of new social media tools become available and increase in sophistication, forensic investigations of terrorist use of social media tools continues to be a challenge. Progress is being made through efforts such as the Dark Web, Check the Web, and the Reynard project, but the law enforcement sees the need for broader and global efforts to combine legal technical and ideological components to the fight against terrorism and its use of social media (CTITF, 2011).

White Collar Crimes

Investigators are commonly using social media sites as part of their investigation of various white collar crimes. For example, insurance companies commonly use social media sites as a source of information related to insurance fraud. Postings that reveal contrary information related to medical claims or claims for property damage provide insurance companies with evidence to use to combat false claims. In one case, a woman testified that she was unemployed due to her injury, but a Facebook posting by her revealed a new job and salary information (Duhl, 2011). However, in most cases, the law prevents insurance investigators from performing more deceptive investigation practices such as "friending" a person under investigation (Duhl, 2011).

In addition to more serious crimes, social media sites have become a common source for information in a wide variety of investigations. Some attorneys are even using social media to gather information about potential jurors (Burdge, 2011). In most cases, this information is publicly available through postings made by social media users, and requires no additional use of forensic tools. If forensic tools are required, the investigator will have to obtain the approval of the legal system to proceed. In all cases, the new court rules allow the attorneys to include requests for social media information and postings in their discovery activities (Walker and Schroeder, 2011).

> Social-networking websites such as Facebook and MySpace have become the go-to places where employers, college admissions officers and divorce lawyers can do background checks. Armed with the information, police have caught fugitives, lawyers have discredited witnesses … and companies have discovered perfect-on-paper applicants engaged in illegal or simply embarrassing behavior
>
> **(Ethics Sage, 2010)**

In addition, social media evidence is being used in civil litigation against large corporation in product liability, personal injury, and employment cases. Social media evidence is also commonly used in copyright and intellectual property cases.

One important point that forensics investigators need to understand is the various laws and regulations that apply in different social media investigation scenarios such as civil litigation claims, crime investigation, and terrorist activity. Investigators need to spend significant time understanding the legal constraints under which they will operate in their social media investigation, before they begin to conduct any investigation.

Summary

We have discussed various social media tools and have also reviewed scenarios in which these social media tools are used to either commit or investigate crimes. A summary chart detailing the social media tool, its use by various parties, and investigation and countermeasure techniques is as follows.

As can be seen in Table 9.1, social media forensic investigation is a combination of an emphasis on both people and data. It relies on both traditional methods of investigation and mastery of current technology and forensic tools. As social media continues to grow in use and volume, it will maintain itself as one of the primary sources of evidence in forensic investigations.

Table 9.1 Social Media Tool Usage Patterns

SOCIAL MEDIA TOOL	STREET GANGS	TERRORIST GROUPS	WHITE COLLAR CRIMES	INVESTIGATION AND COUNTERMEASURES
Social network (e.g., Facebook)	• Communication between members • Planning of crimes • Posting of criminal activity such as photos	• Communication between members of terrorist organizations • Solicitation of new members • Links to other terrorist organizations • Planning of events • Terrorist education such as bomb making and use of weapons • Operational data such as locations for bombs	• Posting of personal information that could reveal the evidence of fraud and other crimes	• Investigation of publicly revealed data • Password identification • Investigation of group member identity • Location, date, and time information through posted photos • Undercover assimilation as group members • Network analysis (e.g., Dark Room)
E-mail and messaging	• Communication between gang members	• Communication between members of terrorist organizations	• Communication that could reveal the evidence of fraud and other crimes	• Identification of e-mail user • Capturing of e-mail during transmission (e.g., wireless access point) • Analysis of e-mail after transmission
Blog		• Spreading of propaganda and solicitation of new members		• Posting of contrary persuasive data • Identification of blog author and responders
Microblogs (e.g., Twitter)	• Communication between members • Planning of crimes • Posting of criminal activity such as photos	• Communication between members of terrorist organizations • Planning of events • Operational data such as locations for bombs	• Communication that could reveal evidence of fraud and other crimes	• Password Identification • Identification of location, date, and time information through posted photos • Undercover assimilation as followers

(Continued)

Table 9.1 (*Continued*)

SOCIAL MEDIA TOOL	STREET GANGS	TERRORIST GROUPS	WHITE COLLAR CRIMES	INVESTIGATION AND COUNTERMEASURES
Location identification	• Posting of presence at locations that could be tied to criminal activity	• Posting of presence at locations that could be tied to terrorist activity	• Posting of presence at locations that could reveal evidence of fraud and other crimes	• Location identification revealed through providers such as Foursquare • Location, date, and time information through posted photos
Event coordination and web conferencing	• Coordination of meetings of gang members	• Coordination of meetings of members of terrorist organizations and sympathizers		• Undercover assimilation as part of group
Multimedia	• Posting of multimedia content that can provide location, time, date, and other information • Posting of multimedia content that can provide the evidence of criminal behavior	• Posting of multimedia content that can provide location, time, date, and other information • Posting of multimedia content that can provide the evidence of terrorist activity • Posting of multimedia content to solicit new members or sympathizers	• Posting of multimedia content that can provide location, time, date, and other potential evidence of fraud and other crimes	• User, location, time, and date available in meta data of posted content
Search	• Searching for contents related to the commission of criminal activities	• Searching for contents related to the commission of terrorist activities	• Searching for contents related to the commission of white collar crimes	• Warrant to search provider to reveal search footprint
Wikis		• Posting of content to solicit new members or sympathizers		• Post contrary information to defuse terrorist organization
Virtual worlds		• Terrorist meetings • Terrorist training activities		• Identify terrorists through behavior modeling • Undercover assimilation as part of group

References

Anglia Ruskin University. (2010). Other Search Engines. Retrieved on July 11, 2011 from http://libweb.anglia.ac.uk/net/othersearch.htm.

Blog@bau. (2011). 20 Useful Specialty Search Engines for College Students. Retrieved on July 10, 2011 from http://bestonlineuniversities.com/2011/20-useful-specialty-search-engines-for-college-students/.

Burdge, R. (2011). New Media in Consumer Transactions and Its Implications. Retrieved on July 29, 2011 from http://dl.dropbox.com/u/6160661/New%20Media%20in%20Consumer%20Transactions%20and%20its%20Implications%202011.pdf.

Counter-Terrorism Implementation Task Force (CTITF). (2011). Countering the Use of the Internet for Terrorism Purposes. Retrieved on July 29, 2011 from http://www.un.org/terrorism/pdfs/CTITF%20Interagency%20WG%20Compendium-%20Legal%20&%20Technical%20Aspects%20WEB.pdf.

Duhl, G. (2011). Social Media and Insurance Fraud. Retrieved on July 29, 2011 from http://web.wmitchell.edu/news/2011/07/social-media-and-insurance-fraud-professor-gregory-duhl-explains/.

Ethics Sage. (2010). Using Social Media to Detect Fraud. Retrieved on July 29, 2011 from http://www.ethicssage.com/2011/07/using-social-media-to-detect-fraud-social-networking-becomes-a-tool-to-detect-fraud-be-careful-what-you-tweet-about-or.html.

Jeffries, A. (2011). Twitter Forensics: Rundown on Evidence Around Rep Weiner. Retrieved on July 28, 2011 from http://www.observer.com/2011/politics/twitter-forensics-rundown-evidence-around-repweiners-crotch-tweet.

KVOA.Com. (2011). UA Researchers Track Terrorists on the "Dark Web." Retrieved on July 29, 2011 from http://www.kvoa.com/news/ua-researchers-track-terrorists-on-the-dark-web-/.

Moilistina, K. (2011). Police Use Facebook to Nab Gang Bangers. Retrieved on July 25, 2011 from http://www.wusa9.com/news/article/139355/77/Police-Use-Facebook-To-Nab-Gang-Bangers.

Mountjoy, B. (2008). When Virtual Meets Reality: WoW, Second Life May Become Targets of Terrorists, CIA. Firefox News. Retrieved on August 18, 2012 from http://firefox.org/news/articles/1580/1/When-Virtual-Meets-Reality-WoW-Second-Life-May-Become-Targets-of-Terrorists-CIA/Page1.html.

Nurwisah, R. (2010). Gangs Using Twitter, Facebook to Plan Crime and Evade Police. Retrieved on July 13, 2011 from http://network.nationalpost.com/np/blogs/posted/archive/2010/02/02/gangs-using-twitter-facebook-to-plan-crimes-evade-police.aspx.

PR Newswire. (2011). Terrorists Using Online Games Undetected by CIA and NSA. Retrieved on July 29, 2011 from http://www.prnewswire.com/news-releases/terrorists-using-online-games-undetected-by-cia-and-nsa-119689779.html.

Public Intelligence. (2010). Terrorist Use of Social Networking Sites. Retrieved on July 28, 2011 from http://publicintelligence.net/ufouoles-dhs-terrorist-use-of-social-networking-facebook-case-study/.

Rafay Hacking Articles. (2010). 4 Ways on How to Hack Facebook Password. Retrieved on July 29, 2011 from http://www.rafayhackingarticles.net/2010/01/4-ways-on-how-to-hack-facebook-password.html.

Ulbricht, M. (2011). Safer Photos: How to Remove Location Infromation From Mobile Images. Retrieved on July 28, 2011 from http://mobileactive.org/howtos/safer-photos-how-remove-location-information-mobile-images.

Walker, R. (2011). Definition of Gangs. Retrieved on July 25, 2011 from http://www.gangsorus.com/definition.html.

Walker, L. & Schroeder, J. (2011). Discovering and Using Social Media in Litigation. Retrieved on July 29, 2011 from http://www.law.com/jsp/cc/PubArticleCC.jsp?id = 1202484355664&Eureka_Discovering_and_Using_Social_Media_in_Litigation.

Washington Times. (2011). Terrorists Discover Uses for Twitter. Retrieved on July 29, 2011 from http://www.washingtontimes.com/news/2011/apr/28/terrorists-discover-uses-for-twitter/?page = 2.

Watkins, T. (2010). Gangs Use of Twitter, Facebook on the Rise. Retrieved on July 13, 2011 from http://www.huffingtonpost.com/2010/02/02/gangs-use-of-twitter-facebook_n_445551.html.

Windows Guides. (2011). EXIF: Your Personal Information Stored in Digital Photos. Retrieved on July 29, 2011 from http://mintywhite.com/more/software-more/exif-personal-information-stored-digital-photos/.

Wondracek, G. H. (2010). A Practical Attack to De-Anonymize Social Network Users. 2010 IEEE Symposium on Security and Privacy, Oakland, CA, USA.

10

SOCIAL ENGINEERING FORENSICS

DR. BARBARA L. CIARAMITARO

Introduction to Social Engineering

> Social Engineering techniques are specifically designed to bypass expensive IT Security countermeasures, which they do often with surprising ease.

> **(Mann, 2008)**

Social Engineering refers to the manipulation of people into releasing information or performing an action. The result of the manipulation is a direct loss of information by the company and/or the achievement of some action that is desired by the social engineering attacker, such as access to computer networks. There are two main approaches that are used by social engineers to perform their attack: technology or human. These are not either/or approaches because social engineers often use a combination of technological and human approaches to persuade their target to release information or perform an action.

There are six main attack vectors commonly used by social engineers to perform their attacks: online, telephone, waste management, mobile devices, personal approaches, and reverse social engineering (Microsoft Technet, 2006).

Online Social Engineering Attacks

One of the most common approaches used in social engineering attacks is the communication through Internet, either through e-mail or websites. The social engineer will use e-mail to persuade a recipient to respond to a request to provide information or access. This may involve false internal e-mails from managers requesting information using *spoofing* techniques to masquerade as the internal manager. Another common technique is to use e-mail to provide an offer of some value to the recipient. When a user responds to this request, he or she is often required to provide information that will allow the social engineer to access to his or her computer system. Alternatively, the online message may provide a link to a website that houses malicious code that will be downloaded to the local computer when the recipient opens the website. Table 10.1 provides an overview of common social engineering online attacks.

TABLE 10.1 Common Social Engineering Online Attacks

ATTACK GOAL	ATTACK VECTOR	ATTACK DESCRIPTION	ATTACK RESULT
Theft of company information	e-mail	Attacker "spoofs" an internal user, vendor, or banking institution to obtain company information.	Unauthorized release of proprietary and confidential information and potential loss of funds.
Theft of personal and company information	e-mail	Attacker sends a "phishing" e-mail that attempts to persuade recipients to reveal personal information that can provide access to personal and company resources.	Attacker is able to achieve unauthorized access to the personal and company computer resources, which can result in unauthorized release of confidential information and loss of funds.
Access to internal computer system	website	Users are persuaded to click a hyperlink and visit a website that will then download malicious software such as key loggers.	Attacker learns usernames and passwords and achieves unauthorized access to the internal computer system.

Telephone Social Engineering Attacks

The telephone is also used by social engineers because it is a familiar medium and protects against any visual identification of them. They are considered to be rather risk free because if the recipient of the call becomes suspicious or noncompliant, then all the social engineers have to hang up. Of course, this is used in combination with calls made through untraceable or public numbers. Social engineers often use the telephone to masquerade as computer support personnel or vendors. They will often use the telephone to persuade frontline employees such as secretaries and receptionists to reveal information about the company. Table 10.2 describes common social engineering telephone attacks.

TABLE 10.2 Common Social Engineering Telephone Attacks

ATTACK GOAL	ATTACK VECTOR	ATTACK DESCRIPTION	ATTACK RESULT
Theft of company information	Phone call to frontline employee	Attacker impersonates an internal employee to gain access to confidential information.	Unauthorized release of proprietary and confidential information and potential loss of funds.
Access to internal computer system	Phone call to help desk	Attacker impersonates an internal employee to have his or her password and access rights changes.	Unauthorized release of proprietary and confidential information and potential loss of funds.
Access to internal computer system	Phone call to internal employee	Attacker impersonates an external vendor or technology provider to gain access to the internal computer system.	Unauthorized release of proprietary and confidential information and potential loss of funds.
Setup for further social engineering attack	Phone call to internal employee	Attacker uses the phone call to set up a future social engineering attack.	Unauthorized release of proprietary and confidential information and potential loss of funds.

TABLE 10.3 Common Social Engineering Waste Management Attacks

ATTACK GOAL	ATTACK VECTOR	ATTACK DESCRIPTION	ATTACK RESULT
Gathering of background information of company	Dumpster diving	The social engineer takes documents, discarded digital media, and other information from externally housed waste containers to obtain background information about the company.	Release of internal organizational structure and identification of employees, access to customer information, and access to confidential or proprietary information.
Gathering of background information of company	Collect documents and information from internal office bins and waste baskets.	The social engineer takes documents, discarded digital media, and other information from internally housed office bins or waste baskets to obtain background information about the company.	Release of internal organizational structure and identification of employees, access to customer information, and access to confidential or proprietary information.

Waste Management Social Engineering Attacks

Social engineers will often use documents and other information discarded by companies as sources of background information for further attacks. This is referred to as "dumpster diving" and can result in the retrieval of a wide variety of important information such as internal organization charts and directories, drafts of proprietary documents, and lists of customers and their identification attributes. Even some shredded documents can be reconstructed by social engineers. Table 10.3 describes common social engineering waste management attacks.

Mobile Device Social Engineering Attacks

Mobile devices have provided new avenues for social engineering attacks. These avenues include *shoulder surfing* of mobile computer users in public places, access to home computer networks, *mobile malware*, and the use of mobile communication devices to impersonate company employees. One growing mobile attack vector is based on the widespread use of applications on mobile devices. This desire for applications has provided social engineers with the opportunity to offer applications that include malicious software designed to install key loggers or other software in the mobile device (Goodchild, 2011b). Once the application is installed, the social engineer can capture user access information to personal sources such as banks and company resources. Public Wi-Fi locations are another playground for social engineers. Social engineers can easily establish a *rogue wireless access point* in a public Wi-Fi location, which will allow them to capture transmissions of the various mobile computing users at that location (Some WiFi, 2011). Another more recent social engineering attack is the use of voice mail messages asking recipients to contact their bank or company (Goodchild, 2010a). This is referred to as *vishing* in that the technique and purpose are similar to e-mail phishing attacks. Table 10.4 describes the common social engineering mobile device attacks.

TABLE 10.4 Common Social Engineering Mobile Device Attacks

ATTACK GOAL	ATTACK VECTOR	ATTACK DESCRIPTION	ATTACK RESULT
Obtaining access to computer system	Shoulder surfing	The social engineer looks over the shoulder of mobile device users at public locations such as airports or Wi-Fi centers and captures their usernames and passwords.	Using the captured username and password, social engineers are able to attain access to the targeted computer system.
Obtaining access to computer system	Home worker	The social engineer masquerades as a support technician to capture the home worker's username and password.	Using the captured username and password, social engineers are able to attain access to the targeted computer system.
Obtaining access to computer system	Mobile applications	The user downloads a mobile game or application that contains malicious software such as key loggers that allow the social engineer to capture usernames and passwords.	Using the captured username and password, social engineers are able to attain access to the targeted computer system.
Capturing wireless transmissions	Rogue Wi-Fi access point	Social engineer establishes a rogue wireless access point in a public Wi-Fi facility to capture computer transmissions including usernames and passwords.	Using the captured username and password, social engineers are able to attain access to the targeted computer system and obtain personal and corporate information.
Obtain personal information	Vishing	Social engineer sends a mobile voicemail message directing the recipient to contact his or her bank or a company.	Capture of personal information and access.

Personal Social Engineering Attacks

Many social engineering attacks are performed in person. These social engineering attacks rely on a number of psychological and cognitive techniques to persuade people to reveal information (Hadnagy, 2010). Four main approaches have proven to be successful techniques for social engineers: intimidation, persuasion, ingratiation, and assistance (Microsoft Technet, 2006). *Intimidation* usually involves the social engineer acting as an authority figure such as a senior executive who "orders" the frontline employ to comply with the request. In some cases, the physical appearance of a social engineer can influence compliance such as when a social engineer dresses as a police officer or a military personnel (Goodchild, 2010a). It is the tendency of most people to try and withdraw from a hostile situation, and as a result using anger can be a very effective social engineering technique (Heary, 2009). *Persuasive* techniques such as flattery, empathy, and name dropping are also effective in gaining compliance. Some social engineering attacks take place over a long period of time, where a social engineer communicates on a regular basis

TABLE 10.5   Common Social Engineering Personal Attacks

ATTACK GOAL	ATTACK VECTOR	ATTACK DESCRIPTION	ATTACK RESULT
Gain access to physical building	Tailgating	Social engineer pretends to be a company employee and follows one or more employees into a building bypassing access controls.	Once a social engineer has achieved internal physical access, they will be able to obtain documents, digital media, and computer access.
Gain computer access	Intimidation, persuasion, ingratiation, or assistance	The social engineer uses one or more psychological and cognitive techniques to obtain compliance from the target.	Access to computer resources, company information, and potential loss of funds.
Gain computer access	Alternative technique	Social engineers use unexpected or alternative techniques such as windshield flyers to lure targets into accessing a malicious website.	Gain access to personal information and resources.

with an employee to establish a relationship. No information is requested while this relationship building is taking place until the final request is made (Mann, 2008). These are referred to as *ingratiation* attacks. The last approach is *providing help or assistance* to the target such as impersonating a support technician. In one example case, a social engineer purchased a Cisco T-shirt on the Internet and used it to gain access to a company as a Cisco technician on a support visit. Once inside, he "dropped" various USB drives laden with malware and was able to access the corporate network. All of this was done in clear view of legitimate company employees (Goodchild, 2010a).

It is important to realize that experienced social engineers are very adept at reading body language and using various techniques to establish a nonverbal connection with the target (Hadnagy, 2010; Heary, 2009). As 55% of communication between humans is nonverbal, this is a very effective ploy (Heathfield, 2011). In addition, social engineers commonly use unexpected and alternative approaches to complete their attack. One example is the use of windshield flyers to persuade people to log on to certain websites for more information (Goodchild, 2010a). Personal social engineering depends on the trusting and helpful nature of humans to be successful. As a result, many people are not even aware that they have been a target of a social engineering attack. Table 10.5 describes common social engineering personal attacks.

Reverse Social Engineering Attacks

Reverse social engineering refers to a situation where a target approaches the social engineer and offers information. This often occurs when the target believes he or she is communicating with a support personnel and therefore above suspicion (Microsoft Technet, 2006). When faced with a computer or account problem, many people will provide access and personal information to the support technician without being

TABLE 10.6   Common Social Engineering Reverse Engineer Attacks

ATTACK GOAL	ATTACK VECTOR	ATTACK DESCRIPTION	ATTACK RESULT
Identity theft	Telephone	The social engineer receives the username and password of a target being "assisted."	Access to personal and company information.
Information theft	Telephone	Using the username and password provided by the target, the social engineer is able to gain access into the internal computer system.	Access to computer resources, company information, and potential loss of funds.
Malicious software	Telephone	A target is persuaded to access an Internet link or download an attachment to help resolve the problem.	The Internet site or attachment contains malicious software that infects the company computer system or installs software such as a key logger or root kit.

asked for it. In some situations, the social engineer will create an environment for this to occur. For example, a social engineer impersonating a support technician may move a file for which a target requires access. The target then requests assistance from the social engineer and provides access and personal information to help resolve the problem. Once this access and personal information has been captured, the social engineer simply replaces the file and the target has no idea that they have just been hacked. Similarly, when social engineers masquerade as law enforcement or military personnel, they are often very successful at persuading people to reveal information to them. Table 10.6 describes the common social engineering reverse engineer attacks.

Using one or more of the techniques described earlier, a summary of common types of social engineering attacks is given as follows:

- *Pretexting* involves creating and using an invented scenario (the pretext) to persuade a victim to release information or perform an action. It is typically done over the telephone and usually involves more than a simple lie. It is often preceded by prior research to successfully use pieces of known information to support the impersonation (e.g., DOB, ss#, and last bill amount) and establish legitimacy in the mind of the target. This technique is often used to trick a business into disclosing customer information from junior company representatives (Federal Trade Commission, 2009).

- *Phishing* is a technique of fraudulently obtaining private information. It is often done through e-mail where the social engineer sends an e-mail that appears to come from a legitimate business—a bank or credit card company—requesting "verification" of information and warning of some dire consequence if it is not provided. The e-mail usually contains a link to a fraudulent web page that seems legitimate—with company logos and content—and has a form requesting everything from a home address to an ATM card's PIN (Microsoft Safety and Security Center, 2011).

- *Baiting* is like the real-world Trojan horse that uses physical media and relies on the curiosity or greed of the victim. In this attack, the attacker leaves a malware-infected floppy disk, CD ROM, or USB flash drive in a location sure to be found (bathroom, elevator, sidewalk, and parking lot), gives it a legitimate looking as well as curiosity-piquing label, and simply waits for the victim to use the device. For example, an attacker might create a CD that is labeled with a corporate logo and label it with "Executive Salary Summary Q2 2009" on the front. An employee would then find it and almost certainly insert the disk into a computer to satisfy his or her curiosity. When installed, the malware would then infect the organization's computer system (Hadnagy, 2010).
- *Quid pro quo* means something for something. In a Quid pro quo attack, an attacker may call random numbers at a company claiming to be calling back from technical support. Eventually, they will hit someone with a legitimate problem, grateful that someone is calling back to help them. The attacker will "help" solve the problem, and in the process have the user type commands that give the attacker access or launch malware (Social Engineering, 2007).
- In a 2003 information security survey, 90% of office workers gave researchers their usernames and passwords in answer to a survey question in exchange for a cheap pen (Leyden, 2003). Similar surveys in later years obtained similar results using chocolates and other cheap lures (BBC News, 2004; Leyden, 2008).
- *Tailgating or piggybacking* refers to the situation when a person tags along with another person who is authorized to gain entry into a restricted area or pass a certain checkpoint. Tailgaters have various methods of breeching security as follows:
  - Following an individual authorized to enter a location, giving the appearance of being legitimately escorted
  - Joining a large crowd authorized to enter and pretending to be a member of the crowd that is largely unchecked
  - Finding an authorized person who either carelessly disregards the rules of the facility or is tricked into believing the tailgater is authorized and agreeably allows the tailgater to tag along

As can be seen from the discussion mentioned earlier, the most difficult aspect of investigating social engineering incidents is their insidious nature. In many cases, it is difficult to even recognize that an incident has occurred. The advantages of the Internet and the breadth and range of communication technologies provide the social engineer with the cover of distance and anonymity. This makes the identification of the attacker difficult in many cases.

To attack your organization, social engineering hackers exploit the credulity, laziness, good manners, or even enthusiasm of your staff. Therefore it is difficult to defend against a social engineered attack, because the targets many not realized that they have been duped....

(Microsoft Technet, 2006)

Social Engineering Forensics

As discussed earlier, investigating social engineering attacks after they have occurred can be quite frustrating for a forensic investigator. Therefore, the best way to handle social engineering attacks is by preventing them in the first place through extensive education and training programs and identification and resolution of vulnerabilities. However, the difficulty of investigating social engineering attacks should not stop the forensic investigator from proceeding.

One of the challenges of investigating social engineering attacks is the type of preparation conducted prior to the actual attack. Social engineers often take weeks or months to gather information on a potential target. Using many of the techniques described earlier, social engineers will gather background information about a company and its employees. They then use this information to conduct their various attacks. Their apparent knowledge of the company and its employees are the successful techniques to gain the trust of their targets (Goodchild, 2010b).

The first step to investigating social engineering attacks is to gain an understanding of the areas of weakness in the organization by doing a vulnerability assessment. This process involves identifying the various social engineering threats and matching them against the existing policies and configurations to determine the areas of vulnerability. If, for example, there is an identified threat of the loss of company proprietary or confidential information through social engineering attacks, the next step would be to determine whether there are any countermeasures in place that would prevent this from occurring. If security countermeasures are in place that can prevent an internal employee from transmitting confidential or proprietary information based on the classification of that information, the forensic investigator now knows that the loss occurred in some other fashion (Mann, 2008). Similarly, if the access to the Internet is limited, then investigations into social engineering attacks using the Internet can be narrowed to those individuals with Internet access. The review of Internet access logs is also valuable in determining who had access to which sites and performed which actions. The use of up-to-date virus protection software can also eliminate e-mail attachments and website downloads as sources of malware infection. As seen by these examples, the first job of the forensic investigator is to narrow the potential attack vectors by examining the current vulnerability and countermeasures. Table 10.7 details the potential attack vulnerabilities.

TABLE 10.7   Social Engineering Attack Vector Vulnerabilities

ATTACK VECTOR	TYPE OF ATTACK	DESCRIPTION	COUNTERMEASURES
Online	E-mail	Malicious attachments	Maintain up-to-date virus protection
	E-mail	Phishing	Education and awareness training
	E-mail	Sending company documents through e-mail	Data loss prevention policy and monitoring and prevention technology
	Website	Malicious downloads	Maintain up-to-date virus protection and limit access to Internet
Phone	Calls to help desk	Persuade help desk technicians to "assist" social engineer caller in resetting password	Extensive training of help desk employees with supporting policies
	Vishing	Persuading voice mail recipients to call a number to reveal information	Education and awareness training
Waste management	Internal document collection	Gathering documents and other information from internal offices	Establish clean desk and document destruction policy
	External document collection	Gathering documents and other information from external waste receptacles	Move dumpsters on site
Physical security	Tailgating	Follow a legitimate employee into the building	Establish strict physical access controls that require all users to show and use their access cards
	Access to offices and computer rooms	Unlocked offices allow access to internal offices and computer rooms	Lock unoccupied offices and computer rooms
People	Persuasion, intimidation, ingratiation, and assistance	Social engineers use a variety of psychological ploys to gain compliance	Education and training programs
	Masquerading as vendor or support personnel	Social engineers will dress and act as external vendor or support technicians to gain access and compliance	Establishing the policy of validating all external visits

Social Engineering Attack Vector Vulnerabilities

The next step is to assess the personnel strength of employees in terms of their resistance to social engineering attacks. If social engineering training and education have taken place, then the more common social engineering attacks may not be successful and more sophisticated attacks may need to be explored. In addition, if there are strict policies in place that induce employees to act accordingly based on consequences, thereby reducing compliance, the chance of certain social engineering attacks such as revealing passwords or physical access may be minimized. Forensic investigations of social engineering attacks should also focus on common attack and entry points such as e-mail, phone calls, websites, frontline employees, and support as well as help desk technicians. Logs of visitors, vendors, and technicians should also be reviewed and validated. In addition, any visits by external support technicians should be traced back to legitimate requests. If none are found, this attack approach should be further investigated. Although vulnerability mapping does not always provide a direct solution to finding the cause of social engineering attacks, they can reduce the potential number of attack vectors to consider.

As mentioned previously, social engineering attacks occur in two ways: through technology and human contact, and often a combination of both. When examining the technology side of a social engineering attack, it is necessary to back trace the various steps used to access the computer system. In situations where the attack began through an e-mail message, for example, the first step is to back trace that message to its source. This is done by tracking the e-mail headers through their various transmission points (Online Tech Tips, 2007). In the case of malware being introduced into the organization, the investigator must explore the various entry points such as e-mail attachments, websites, mobile devices, and peripheral devices such as USB drives. If the malware can be traced to its source entry machine, the investigator has a good chance of discovering its origin and potentially back tracing its source and method of introduction.

When investigating human attacks, the forensic investigators can utilize various approaches. In some cases, it may be worthwhile to determine who would be most vulnerable at the company to revealing information. This could include a review of the organizational structure, roles of frontline employees, employees with mobile access, vacation schedules, and history of technician service calls or other visitors to the facility. If a company utilizes a video recording of entry and access points, it may be possible to identify individuals who have tailgated their way into the building.

Forensic analysis of social engineering attacks requires the investigator to be versatile in his or her techniques employing both technical analysis, along with an understanding of human behavior. Understanding the current environment and its limitations are the required first step. Understanding the corporate culture as well as the roles and responsibilities can also prove helpful. The analysis of a social engineering attack is rarely straightforward and may take many steps in a variety of technical and nontechnical areas to complete.

Conclusion

Social Engineering attacks have been quite successful in several recent well-publicized incidents. Their success, even against well-protected companies and the military, demonstrates the challenges the organizations face in preventing social engineering attacks. These examples also illustrate the challenges faced by the forensic investigators of social engineering attacks. (Goodchild, 2011a).

- *Wikileaks* is one example of a social engineering attack conducted by an insider to obtain confidential and secret information. U.S. Army Private Bradley Manning is accused of accessing internal sources of information and passing that information to Julian Assange, the founder of Wikileaks. "He allegedly managed to fool colleagues into thinking he was listening to music, rather than steeling classified information ..." (Goodchild, 2011a).
- *Google Hack* involved the breaching of Google customer information to access Gmail accounts of Chinese human-rights activists. The Chinese social engineers apparently accomplished their attack by "carrying out a length reconnaissance of Google employees" (Goodchild, 2011a). They sent what appeared as legitimate messages to Google employees who clicked on an embedded link that installed spyware on to their computers.
- *Facebook* scams are very common and occur almost daily in which social engineers post links to malware-infected sites urging Facebook "friends" to click on those links and install the software.
- The attack on *RSA* began with phishing e-mails with attached files sent to a selected group of employees within RSA. The e-mail was titled "2011 Recruitment Plan." Even though this e-mail was automatically sent to the users' junk mail file, one employee retrieved the e-mail and opened the attachment. "The spreadsheet contained malware that used a previously unknown, or 'zero-day,' flaw in Adobe's Flash software to install a backdoor" (Richmond, 2011, p. 1).
- *Booz Allen* suffered a similar fate when a targeted spear phishing attack induced one of its employees to open an e-mail with a malware-infected attachment. Once again, the social engineers were able to use this malware to access the Booz Allen system (Panataleon, 2011).

References

BBC News. (2004). Passwords Revealed by Sweet Deal. Retrieved on July 29, 2011 from http://news.bbc.co.uk/2/hi/technology/3639679.stm.

Federal Trade Commission. (2009). Pretexting: Your Personal Information Revealed. Retrieved on July 29, 2011 from http://www.ftc.gov/bcp/edu/pubs/consumer/credit/cre10.shtm.

Goodchild, J. (2010a). Social Engineering Techniques: 4 Ways Criminal Outsiders Get Inside. Retrieved on July 30, 2011 from http://www.csoonline.com/article/596512/social-engineering-techniques-4-ways-criminal-outsiders-get-inside.

Goodchild, J. (2010b). Social Engineering: The Basics. Retrieved on July 29, 2011 from http://www.csoonline.com/article/print/514063.

Goodchild, J. (2011a). Social Engineering Attacks: Highlights from 2010. Retrieved on July 29, 2011 from http://www.csoonline.com/article/print/651490.

Goodchild, J. (2011b). Three Social Engineering Tricks Hackers are Using to Compromise Mobile Devices. Retrieved on July 28, 2011 from http://www.computerworlduk.com/advice/security/3293477/three-social-engineering-tricks-hackers-are-using-to-compromise-mobile-devices/.

Hadnagy, C. A. (2010). *Social Engineering: The Art of Human Hacking.* Wiley.

Heary, J. (2009). Top 5 Social Engineering Exploit Techniques. Retrieved on July 28, 2011 from http://www.pcworld.com/article/182180/top_5_social_engineering_exploit_techniques.html.

Heathfield, S. (2011). Non Verbal Communication. Retrieved on July 29, 2011 from http://humanresources.about.com/od/interpersonalcommunicatio1/a/nonverbal_com.htm.

Leyden, J. (2003). Office Workers Give Away Passwords for a Pen. Retrieved on July 29, 2011 from http://www.theregister.co.uk/2003/04/18/office_workers_give_away_passwords/.

Leyden, J. (2008). Women Love Chocolate More than Password Security. Retrieved on July 29, 2011 from http://www.theregister.co.uk/2008/04/16/password_security/.

Mann, I. (2008). *Hacking the Human.* Gower, Brookfield, Vermont.

Microsoft Safety and Security Center. (2011). What is Phishing? Retrieved on July 29, 2011 from http://www.microsoft.com/security/resources/phishing-whatis.aspx.

Microsoft Technet. (2006). How to Protect Insiders from Social Engineering Threats. Retrieved on July 27, 2011 from http://technet.microsoft.com/en-us/library/cc875841.aspx.

Online Tech Tips. (2007). How to Track the Original Location of an Email via Its IP Address. Retrieved on July 29, 2011 from http://www.online-tech-tips.com/computer-tips/how-to-track-the-original-location-of-an-email-via-its-ip-address/.

Panataleon, E. (2011). Classified Military Information Leaked. Retrieved on July 30, 2011 from http://techmento.com/2011/07/12/classified-military-information-leaked/.

Richmond, R. (2011). The RSA Hacl: How They Did It. Retrieved on July 30, 2011 from http://bits.blogs.nytimes.com/2011/04/02/the-rsa-hack-how-they-did-it/.

Social Engineering. (2007). The Security Tutorial. Retrieved on July 29, 2011 from http://www.securitytutorials3.thetazzone.com/engineering.html.

Some WiFi. (2011). A Guide to How Wifi Works. Retrieved on July 29, 2011 from http://somewifi.com/.

11

ANTI-FORENSICS*

PROF. VELISLAV PAVLOV

Anti-Forensic Definition and Concepts

Before we can dive into exploring the definition of anti-forensics, we need to step back and understand the concept of crime investigation. Dr. Edmond Locard introduced the principle of crime investigation. He stated that when a crime is committed, there is a cross-transfer of evidence between the crime scene and the perpetrator. During a forensic investigation, we deploy science to reveal the transferred evidence and decipher its meaning. The examination process requires that the evidence is reliable and accurate (Harris, 2006).

In the world of digital forensics, evidence resides mainly on the computer storage devices in the form of files, logs, registry key entries, and other "elements" portraying a particular activity. Let us contrast Locard's principle to the digital world. We have two "Windows computers" called computer A and computer B. Map a share from computer A to computer B. Given that we have our audit policies set properly, we should have a login entry in the "Security Event Log." If we use the "net session" command on computer B, we should see the IP of computer A. On the contrary, if we type "net use" on computer A, the information about computer B should be displayed. Relating the example to Locard's principle of crime investigation, one computer could be the "crime scene" and the other could be the "perpetrator." Evidence of our computer activity was left behind on both the computers, which could be used in a digital forensic investigation.

What is anti-forensics? Newton's third law of motion states that "for every action there is an equal and opposite reaction." If forensics is the "application of science to those criminal and civil laws which are enforced by police agencies in a criminal justice system," then "anti-forensics" is the opposite (Harris, 2006). Garfinkel (2007) outlined that anti-forensics is "tools and techniques that frustrate forensic tools, investigations, and investigators." On the other hand, Peron and Legary (2005) defined

---

* *Disclaimer of Liability:* The content of this chapter is for information and educational purposes only, and may not be used in any illegal, unethical, immoral, or otherwise malicious manner. Neither the publisher nor authors shall be liable for any loses, injuries, and other damages resulting from the use or misuse of this chapter.

anti-forensics as "the attempt to limit the identification, collection, collation, and validation of electronic data." Others define anti-forensics simply as techniques to avoid detection or hiding of system intrusion. There is a wide variety of interpretation for the definition of anti-forensics. For the purpose of this chapter, anti-forensics will be defined as "any attempt to compromise the availability or usefulness of evidence during the forensics process" (Harris, 2006).

Why anti-forensics? Anti-forensics has a wide range of application areas and purposes. The areas are as broad as our human imagination. It is similar to asking why people hack computers. The main purpose of anti-forensics is to antagonize forensics. We could only speculate what the real "need" for anti-forensics is. Some probabilities or rather assumptions are as follows:

- *Protect privacy:* Some people believe in their privacy at home.
- *Protect assets and intellectual property:* For example, encryption and digital watermarking.
- *Safeguard national security:* Anti-forensics might be useful to protect secret government documents or hide traces of top secret operations.
- *Espionage:* Anti-forensics might play an important role in national, international, and corporate intelligence operations.
- *Defend criminal activity:* Hide traces of wrongdoing.
- *Nurture cyber warfare:* Hacktivism, political power, and supremacy.

Anti-Forensic Methods

Often, there is more than one way to perform a task. The same is valid for conducting anti-forensics. In this section, we will address some of the anti-forensic methods, and we will categorize them according to their purpose vector. Just as we witnessed with the definition of anti-forensics, there are different perceptions of categorizing the anti-forensic methods. Peron and Legary (2005), Rogers (2005), and Harris (2006) proposed their views of categorization. Table 11.1 introduces a side-by-side comparison of the three approaches.

If we take a close look at the three different categorizations, we should notice apparent similarities. Anti-forensic methods aim to hide, destroy, confuse, and otherwise minimize or eliminate the source of evidence. Let us examine some basic examples of each category. By eliminating the source (footprint), we could eliminate the related evidence.

Table 11.1 Categorizing Anti-Forensic Methods

PERON AND LEGARY	ROGERS	HARRIS
Hiding	Data hiding	Hiding data
Destroying	Artifact wiping	Destroying data
Preventing from being created	Attacks against the process and tools	Elimination of source
Manipulating	Trail obfuscation	Counterfeiting

Hiding refers to placing files inside other files or making the files unreadable by the means of encryption. Destroying pertains to irreversible erasing or overwriting of file content. Confusing is the act of overwriting file content with misleading information. It is important to note that some anti-forensic methods could be multipurpose. For example, if we deploy anti-forensics to wipe a file, we attempted to destroy data. To the author's knowledge, a standardized categorization of anti-forensics does not exist. For the purpose of this chapter, we will categorize the anti-forensic methods in the following categories:

- Eliminate trails
- Hide evidence
- Destroy evidence

Eliminate Trails

During a digital crime examination, investigators acquire digital image of the analyzed media. A few of the main goals of the forensic process are to find the evidence, collect it, and preserve its original state. On the contrary, the goal of anti-forensics will be to circumvent this process. In this section, we will focus on minimizing or eliminating the source of footprints. One of the easiest approaches is to block access to the digital media (Pajek and Pimenidis, 2009). This could be a physical access limitation like locks, safes, and special insulations obstructing access to the evidence. On the other hand, it could be software/hardware restrictions like prohibiting portable devices and access to certain applications/services via group policies, registry modifications, malware like rootkits, and so on.

In Windows, we could prevent time stamp update of the last time we have accessed the NTFS directory. For this purpose, we could create REG_DWORD entry "NtfsDisableLastAccessUpdate" with property value set to "1" inside "HKLM\System\CurrentControlSet\Control\Filesystem." Although this is arguably the easiest method, it is probably not the most efficient. Experienced forensic investigators will be able to extract the digital storage medium and analyze it outside of the physical host environment, therefore bypassing the physical obstacles set by the native environment.

An alternative anti-forensic technique could be to neutralize the sources of evidence. Wearing gloves could perpetuate the collection of physical fingerprints. In a digital context, we could disable the tools responsible for the creation of audit trails. This could be achieved by exploiting registry settings, group policies, operating system settings, and malware (Pajek and Pimenidis, 2009). In our earlier example of mapping computer A share on computer B, we mentioned that proper security logging needs to be configured. Without the logging in place, we may not be able to collect as much evidence. In Windows, if we ran a "net stop eventlog" command, we could disable the logging service. Therefore, we eliminated or at the least reduced future traces of activity. For Linux/Unix, we could stop the "syslog" daemon to circumvent system logs. It would be critical to note that there may be more than one logging service for the corresponding operating system.

When we visit a website, our browser exchanges information with the web server. Most of the time, the information is revealed without our consent. We could visit http://browserspy.dk or www.my-addr.com, which could help us examine what digital fingerprint we might be revealing to third parties. For example, information like IP, browser information, operating system, and geographical location are exposed instantly. In addition, our browser could remember what sites we have visited, files we have downloaded, form information, and even login credentials. One of the anti-forensic techniques to eliminate the source of this type of information is to change the browser settings not to remember history, credentials, form information or retain cookies and offline files.

Many of the web applications and web servers query our browser by using scripts. For example, JavaScript is enabled by default in most modern browsers. We should note that malicious JavaScript could reveal any asterisk password for any website without our consent. Figure 11.1 illustrates that we have entered a username (ANTI-FORENSICS), and a masked password (It's3@zy2h4k!!). Figure 11.2 shows how easy it is to reveal the password by parsing a simple JavaScript command in the address bar of our browser.

The bottom line is that scripts enable greater functionality within our browser and allow for easy harvesting of forensic data. To eliminate the evidence source, we could disable scripts (JavaScript and CSS) in our browser's settings or configuration files. Most modern browsers offer "Private Browsing" mode, which may not save any browsing information or add-ons.

Last but not least, is it possible not to leave any traces? The answer for this question is debatable; however, the short answer is that it is possible, but not probable. For instance, let us examine memory injection. Buffer overflows allow an attacker to inject and run arbitrary code to address the space of a running application. Thus, the result is changing the behavior of the victim's application. Garfinkel (2007) explained that "userland execve" allows an attacker to load and execute applications on the victim's computer

Figure 11.1   Secure login window.

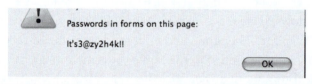

Figure 11.2   Password revealed.

without the use of Unix "execve()" kernel call. In other words, the anti-forensic application allows an attacker to bypass kernel-based security systems that deny access to "execve()" and log its use to a secure logging service.

As a matter of fact, Ripe and Pluf (2005) wrote that "userland execve" is a mechanism which simulates correctly and orderly procedures followed when the kernel loads an executable in memory and then runs it. Garfinkel (2007) added that "userland execve" could be read from a network without being written to the victim's storage medium. Instead of loading an exploit program on the victim's device, the attacker could use "system call proxy" which could accept remote procedure calls from the attacker. The "system call proxy" could also assist to execute the requested procedure call on the victim's device and ultimately report the results back to the attacker. Harris et al. (2008) reported that using "system call proxy" shellcode allows us to run malicious code without any files being uploaded to the target and without the creation of new processes on the target's machine.

Harris et al. (2008) discussed an alternative shellcode technique called "process injection" shellcode. It allows an attacker to load complete libraries of code running under a separate thread of execution within the context of an existing process on the target's computer. In a sense, we are "piggy-back riding" on an existing process. With this approach, we could load code in the existing process without leaving traces of changes on the target machine. Once we have invaded the process, we could "jump" to a different process and migrate our code library if necessary. The injected code may never be written to the storage medium on the target machine. The most well-known tool for the process injection anti-forensic method is Meterpreter advanced payload included in the Metasploit Framework (www.metasploit.com).

This section will be incomplete if did not mention live CDs, portable storage devices, and virtual machines. These approaches allow us to run a variety of applications while significantly reducing the sources of evidence footprint. Let us take a look at each approach:

- *Live CDs:*
  - All-in-one live CDs: Portable operating system distribution and tools running from read-only disks. They have graphical user interface and tend to run with virtual memory disabled (Garfinkel, 2007). They are equipped with heavy artillery of tools for pen testing, forensics/anti-forensics, anonymous browsing, and so on. Some examples are BackTrack, Helix, Hiren, Metasploit MAFIA, PHLAK, Auditor, Knoppix-STD, and UBCD4Win.
  - Anonymous browsing live CDs: Light operating system distribution specifically designed for anonymous web browsing. A few examples are Anonym.OS, Polippix, Sabayon, and Privatix.
- *Bootable USB tokens:* Most of the live CDs have the ability to be installed to a portable storage device instead burned to a CD/DVD. The USB storage

could be configured as writable in comparison with read-only mode in the Live CD approach.

- *Virtual machines:* The operating system or program runs within a virtual environment. This could be to an attacker's advantage since some security tools may not look for a "rootkit" running in a virtual environment. The virtual machine saves its state to files on the storage medium of the physical host.

Last but not least, we need to mention anonymous accounts. We could use fake identities and storage from public sources (e.g., Yahoo!, Gmail, ADrive, Dropbox) to avoid storage information and tool evidence on local computers. In addition, websites like www.bugmenot.com, http://www.phenoelit-us.org/dpl/dpl.html, and http://10minutemail.com offer generic account credentials, default device passwords, and temporary e-mail address to the public mass. Such resources could help to minimize the source for evidence of footprint in a digital forensic investigation.

Hide Evidence

If we cannot eliminate the evidence, we could attempt to remove it from plain view/ hide it. This technique does not attempt to destroy or manipulate the evidence. It is an attempt to make it less visible during the forensic investigation process. It is important to note that hiding of the evidence is almost as important as hiding tools. If the investigator detects the presence of a "hiding" tool, this discovery alone could become incriminating evidence (Harris, 2006).

The success of hiding depends on the people factor. There is no guarantee that hiding the evidence will be successful. We could hope that we hid the evidence in a place which the investigator might overlook. Hiding as an anti-forensic technique also takes advantage of the limitations of the physical and the digital world. Files could be hidden in "plain sight" to exploit investigator's blind spots or within other files to exploit the inherited limitations of the forensics software (Harris, 2006).

Indeed, cryptography is one such approach which enables us to effectively hide information. However, it is important to note that cryptography does not address the fact that encrypted data is easy to spot by forensic tools. Garfinkel (2007) noted that encrypted data has unusually high entropy; many encryption tools embed certain flags, headers, and signatures, which aid the forensic tools to discover the encrypted data. Even encryption of the hidden data is possible if the investigator retrieves the encryption key.

There are different encryption approaches. One of them is cryptographic file system. Cryptographic file systems transparently encrypt data as the data is written to the disk. The data could become inaccessible if the cryptographic key is destroyed. For example, the creators (http://usbsafeguard.altervista.org) of the "USB Safeguard" application claim that it encrypts the data with AES 256-bit and the password protects USB drives. The creators also mentioned that if we entered the access password incorrectly "X" number of times, the data would be destroyed.

On the other hand, Mah (2007) wrote about "IronKey" from www.ironkey.com, which claims the product is the world's most secure flash drive. It offers hardware-based AES 256-bit encryption, optional anti-malware, and hardware level overwriting of data if the password was not typed correctly 10 times. The keys for the encryption are hardware generated by a FIPS 140-2 compliant True Random Number Generator.

In addition to encryption file systems and software, we need to address encrypted network protocols like SSL/TLS and SSH. Since most people should be familiar with either, we will talk about I2P, which is known as the "anonymous network" (www.i2p2.de). The network built in order to aid our free society by offering uncensorable, anonymous, and secure communication. I2P routes traffic through other peers where traffic is encrypted several times from end-to-end. A variety of mail, peer-to-peer, and IRC applications support I2P. It would be preposterous to claim that I2P provides 100% anonymity. The point here is that it could obstruct the forensic analysis; therefore, it deserves mention in the anti-forensic tools and techniques chapter. Figure 11.3 from the author's website shows the traffic encryption process from Alice to Bob.

In the addition, when we talk about hiding and anti-forensics, we need to mention the infamous "Tor project" from www.torproject.org. Tor helps us to hide among other users on the network. The more people on the network, the harder it will be to analyze our traffic. According to information found on the Tor website, Tor protects the user by distributing the user transactions over multiple places on the Internet. Therefore, no single point could link us to our destination. Instead of going directly from "A" to "B" like we would with I2P, we travel a random pathway through multiple relays to cover our tracks. Determining where data came from or where data is destined to go is very difficult to trace.

In fact, Geelkerken (2006) explained that Tor uses a technique called anonymizing proxy. The anonymizer proxy is a server, which reroutes requests from one location to another. In addition, Tor uses a variation of digital mixing. Digital mixing is like sending a letter encased in four different envelopes which are pre-addressed and prestamped with a tiny message "please remove this envelop and repost." If the next three recipients repost the letter, the letter would reach the intended recipient without leaving a paper

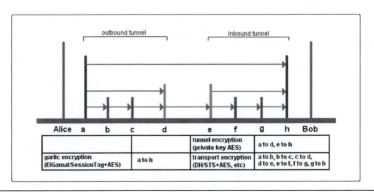

Figure 11.3 I2P encrypted traffic flow.

Figure 11.4 Digital mixing: Alice sends a message to Bob.

trail between the first sender and the final recipient. Figure 11.4 outlines the digital mixing process by having Alice send a message to Bob. Alice would encrypt her message to Bob three times with a public key cryptography. She would then send the message to a proxy server, which will remove the first key. The second and third server will decrypt and permute the message each by using one of the remaining two keys until the message is sent to Bob.

In addition to encrypted networks like I2P and Tor, program packers could be an effective hiding technique against anti-forensics. Packers are used to hide tools from reverse engineering or forensic detection by scanning. Packers like PECompact from www.bit-sum.com could be used to encrypt/compress and wrap our tool with a suitable extractor. Packers could also be used against debugging (Garfinkel, 2007). UPX (http://upx.source-forge.net) is a free executable packer supporting different formats like OS X executable, Windows x32-bit executables, Linux shell script, and so on. These file joiners for instance could help join a malicious code inside an EXE, PDF, JPG, MP3 or other files. For instance, if we take an innocent program and malicious program, we could join them into a new program. During the joining process, we could specify if we want to hide the malicious program before or after the execution of the innocent program. Even Windows offers a build-in tool, IExpress, which could allow us to pack/join executable files.

According to Pajek and Pimenidis (2009), data could also be hidden in unallocated, unusual or hard to reach locations. Manipulating file extensions, headers, and footers could mislead forensic analysis tools. Other approaches could be to use hidden partitions, nested directories, and slack space. Data on hard disks is saved in clusters, which are separated in sectors. Information like file name, size, and time stamp are stored on the hard drive. Saved data might not use all sectors in a dedicated cluster, which in return offers additional hiding places. Garfinkel (2007) added that Metasploit's Slacker, part of MAFIA distro, allows hiding files with the slack space of NTFS file systems. Retrieving the hidden data is possible via the reverse algorithm supplied by Slacker.

When we talk about hiding data, we should also mention "TrueCrypt." Available through www.truecrypt.com, it offers on-the-fly disk encryption through algorithms like AES, Twofish, Serpent, combined algorithm variations, and so on. With this application, we could create nested files/directories and encrypt entire hard disks and portable storage devices. We could store our most important data inside several hidden volumes. Each volume has an individual volume password; we unlock a volume based on the password we specified. We could think of the hidden nested volumes as layers of protection. The most important data could lay in the inner most volume. If someone challenges us to reveal our hidden data, we could reveal the least significant information without jeopardizing the inner most volume with the most critical data.

TrueCrypt's hidden-nested volumes lead us to steganography as an alternative approach to hiding data from forensic tools. The primary purpose of steganography is the concealment of information or making it invisible to the human eye. It differs from encryption in the sense that encryption makes the information unreadable. Steganography relies on the human perception. Human sense could be inadequate to detect information concealed in an innocent looking image, audio, video file or just about any file format (McGill, 2005). There are many concealment tools available on the Web. Johnson (2011) provided an extensive list of tools at http://www.jjtc.com/Steganography/tools.html. McGill (2005) explained that there are three main steganography approaches:

1. *Substitution:* Using the least significant bit (LSB) approach where if we replace the last bit in a byte, its changes will be insignificant for detection by the human eye.
2. *Injection:* Used to literally inject the secret message into the carrier file. In audio files, we could hide the message within a noise signal where the message is scattered across broad frequency spectrum. Alternatively, we could inject a message by adding echo to a signal, which varies by amplitude, decay rate, and offset.
3. *Generation of new files:* In this approach, we take the secret message and use it to generate a file from scratch. A good example would be www.spammmimic.com. The service encodes a message like "anti-forensics" into innocently looking garbage message (spam).

For example,

Dear Friend, You made the right decision when you signed up for our club. If you no longer wish to receive our publications simply reply with a Subject: of "REMOVE" and you will immediately be removed from our mailing list. This mail is being sent in compliance with Senate bill 1624; Title 5; Section 301 ! This is not multi-level marketing ! ...

How many of us would bother reading this garbage message? The person expecting the secret message could decode it using the same web service and receive the secret message "Anti-forensics." Steganography is not just a tool, it is an art and science!

After reviewing steganography, we need to mention alternate data streams (ADS). Zadjmool (2004) explained that ADS is a feature of any version of the Windows NTFS (file system). It is a method of hiding rootkits or hacker tools on a compromised system and executing these tools without being noticed. What ADS does is, it offers the ability to append file data into existing files without affecting their functionality, size, or visual presentation. For example, if we type:

"C:\Forensics> echo "ANTIFORENSICS are DANGEROUS" > file.txt:hidden.txt", we just added ADS to "file.txt" called "hidden.txt." The colon ":" separates the

ADS and the carrier file. If we list the content of the container folder, the hidden ADS will not be revealed. Please review the following example:

```
C:\Forensics>echo "ANTIFORENSICS are DANGEROUS" > file.txt:hidden.txt
C:\Forensics>dir
Volume in drive C has no label.
Volume Serial Number is XXXX-XXXX
Directory of C:\Forensics
05/27/2011 10:19 PM <DIR>  .
05/27/2011 10:19 PM <DIR>  ..
05/27/2011 10:19 PM 0 file.txt
  1 File(s)  0 bytes
  2 Dir(s) 30,437,232,640 bytes free
```

In this example, we injected a secret message "ANTIFORENSICS are DANGEROUS" inside the ADS (hidden.txt) not the file.txt. If we open "file.txt," it will be blank (size "0"). Using Helios Lite, LADS or an alternative ADS revealing tool, we could reveal that the file "file.txt:hidden.txt" indeed is "27 bytes."

```
C:\Forensics>lads LADS - Freeware version 4.10
(C) Copyright 1998-2007 Frank Heyne Software (http://www.heysoft.de)
This program lists files with alternate data streams (ADS)
Use LADS on your own risk!
Scanning directory C:\Forensics\
size ADS in file
- - - - - - - - - - - - - - - - - - - - - - - - - - - - - - - - - - - -
27 C:\Forensics\file.txt:hidden.txt
27 bytes in 1 ADS listed
```

The ADS segment preludes us to rootkits. Rootkits, in brief, are often associated with a compilation of hacking tools like Trojans, backdoors, remote administration, and downloader malware, which invades a target system and hides its presence from the user and known security software. Some popular variations are Hacker Defender, t0rnkit, Adore, b0stt, and so on. Milliron (2010) reported that rootkits operate at the highest privilege level, the kernel, which is also where the operating system (OS) functions. The difference with Trojans is that Trojans run at Ring 3, which is most commonly associated with application operation. Rootkits operate as part of the OS instead of just being an application on top of the OS. There are various infection vector techniques:

- *MBR infection:* The Master Boot Record tells the BIOS (Basic Input Output System) where to find the OS. MBR rootkits could insert themselves between the hardware and the OS. When the OS interacts with the hard drive, the rootkit could intercept and manipulate the communication to execute malicious code or hide its presence.
- *Hypervisor:* It could be defined as the virtual machine manager allowing for a single physical system to host multiple guest systems. It simulates hardware

operations, intercepts OS requests, translates them, and passes them to the physical hardware. Hypervisor rootkits could modify the bootloader to create malicious hypervisor similar to MBR infection or subvert the OS and migrate it to a virtual machine while it is still running. The rootkit could gain control of what the OS sees, which means that it could be extremely difficult to detect.

- *Alternate data streams:* This is rootkit utopia since ADS are not viewable without special software by the human eye and there is no limit on the number or size of files, which can be stored in ADS.
- *Slack space:* Rootkits could hide in slack space, because it is one of the areas many security tools cannot effectively scan.
- *Interrupt hooks:* IRQ or interrupt requests are used by the OS uses to interface with the system hardware. A rootkit, which could intercept these requests are known to have hooks. In other words, the rootkit has a control of the hardware at a very low level. For example, the INT 13h enables direct access to the hard drive. This means that a rootkit could gain direct access control and modify the disk.
- *Message hooks:* Application executed in memory use messages to communicate modification and user input to other programs and the OS. Message hooks are used to monitor or intercept messages before they reach a destination process. The benefit of this approach is that a rootkit will be able to intercept all user activity on the system. For example, WH_KEYBOARD, WH_KEYBOARD_LL, and WH_MOUSE are common messages hooks used by rootkits.
- *SSDT hooks:* The OS uses System Service Descriptor Table (SSDT) to locate system-critical services. If a rootkit has a control over SSDT, any program, which tries to use SSDT will be rerouted through the rootkit. For example if NtQueryDirectoryFile is hooked, the rootkit could give false information to anti-malware tool.
- *IRP hooks:* I/O request packets (IRPs) is used every time a program communicates with the system hardware. For example, reading/writing data from a hard drive, RAM, video, and network are all associated with IRP. IRP hooks involve changing hardware drivers. For example, if a rootkit controls tcpip.sys, it could hide network traffic.
- *DKOM:* Direct kernel object manipulation (DKOM) allows rootkits to access kernel objects directly. It allows the rootkit to make system changes, which are only occurring in memory, making the rootkit virtually undetectable. DKOM control also allows the rootkit to stay undetected because the many anti-malware tools cannot access the kernel objects.

Destroy Evidence

After we discussed some methods for anti-forensic hiding methods, we will now shift focus to methods to destroy evidence or information. Harris (2006) wrote that evidence destruction refers to the process of the dismantling or otherwise making the evidence unusable. It completely wipes out the evidence or information. For example, digital data destruction could be compared to wiping off fingerprints.

Most of us probably are aware that we cannot really erase data. Instead, we could overwrite it. Garfinkel (2007) points out that there are different approaches to overwriting data. We could have a program to overwrite the entire storage media or individual files. For example, Ciphter.exe on Windows platforms could overwrite data with a pass of zeros, a pass of FF's, and a pass of random data. Apple's Disk Utility offers us to overwrite data with a single pass (NULL bytes) and seven passes or 35 passes (Gutman's pass) of random data. The problem is not the method; the problem is which data to overwrite. Overwriting an entire drive is relatively easy with tools like DBAN (Darik's Boot Nuke), Active KillDisk, Disk Wipe, SFill, Srm, and others. The problem is that the wiping tool might leave data and fingerprints that the tool was used on the system.

Instead of drawing attention to wiping a file, we could overwrite the file's metadata like access, creation, and modification time stamps. Overwriting metadata was described by Garfinkel (2007) as the process of overwriting file attributes. For example, the examiner could attempt to construct activity timeline. Forensic tool could be deployed to analyze file time stamps in a chronological order. Metasploit's time stamp allows manipulating NTFS create, modify, access, and delete time stamps. On Unix boxes, Defiler's toolkit or the touch command could be used to overwrite time stamps.

Mobile Anti-Forensics

According to statistics, there are at least 2.6 billion mobile subscribers in the world. China Mobile reported that it is adding 6 million new subscribers per month. Today, mobile devices are compact computers. Mobile devices are armed with graphical interface, computational resources, and connectivity. More personal information is being stored on such devices making them a perfect target for forensic analysis (Distefano et al., 2010). Some of the traditional anti-forensic techniques may not be applicable to the mobile world. The need for anti-forensic tools is eminent for many reasons. Let us take a closer look at anti-forensic techniques for the Android OS.

There are different anti-forensic techniques for the Android mobile platform described by Distefano et al. (2010):

- *Mobile internal acquisition tool (MIAT):* Putting ourselves in the shoes of the investigator could help us formulate better anti-forensic plan. MIAT is an open source mobile forensic application available via http://miatforensics.org. It could be used as a proactive measure of finding evidence/data we left behind.
- *Exploiting Android features:* Android binds any running application to a secure Sandbox, which cannot interfere with other applications without explicit permissions. The permissions are defined once statically during the application installation and do not change during the lifetime of the application.

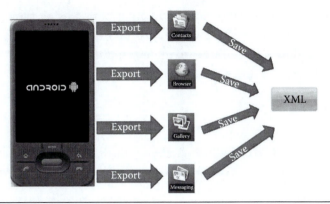

Figure 11.5 Evidence export process on Android platform.

All applications must be signed with developer's certificate to establish interactions with other applications. For example, we could create an application, which protects certain files or folders. The protection then is ensured at OS level; therefore, serving as an anti-forensic technique.

- *Private folder:* We could create a private folder, which is only accessible to the application we specified. This folder could store text files and multimedia to name a few. The folder will be hidden from other applications ensuring a level of steganography.
- *Anti-forensic application:* AFDroid is an application which creates a private folder, but it also allows the execution of two processes:
  - *Evidence export process (EEP):* Exporting information stored on a mobile device to a private location
  - *Evidence import process (EIP):* Reversing the EEP process
- *Evidence export process:* Figure 11.5 illustrates the EEP process where we use AFDroid to export information like text messages and contacts and export it to a secure XML file (private storage).
- *Honeycomb:* It introduced a new API, which supports enforcement of encrypted storage and password protection (Hollister, 2011). Fisher (2011) reported that WhisperCore is an alternative software offering encryption for mobile devices.
- *Evidence destruction:* If we need to destroy our private folder, we simply uninstall the AFDroid application. Use of the factory data reset features built into Android deletes some data, but some data may remain on the device. Additionally, Google's Sync, Kaspersky Mobile Security, and Microsoft Exchange 2010 all offer features to remotely wipe the data on a mobile device.

Conclusion

There are many different tools and techniques that can be employed to confound the forensic examiner. Many of these techniques do present significant challenges and may in fact make it impossible to recover the information using typical forensic practices. Developing an awareness of the way anti-forensic tools and techniques and how they are employed allows an examiner to understand the strengths—and the potential to exploit weaknesses—of anti-forensic practices.

References

Distefano, A., Me, G., and Pace, F. (2010). Android Anti-Forensics Through a Local Paradigm. Retrieved on May 28, 2011 from www.dfrws.org/2010/proceedings/2010-310.pdf

Fisher, D. (2011, March 17). Device Level Encryption Comes to Android. In *Threatpost*. Retrieved on May 28, 2011 from http://threatpost.com/en_us/blogs/device-level-encryption-comes-android-031711

Garfinkel, S. (2007). Anti-Forensics: Techniques, Detection and Countermeasures. Retrieved on May 28, 2011 from http://www.simson.net/clips/academic/2007.ICIW.AntiForensics.pdf

Geelkerken, F. W. (2006, December 1). Tor: The Onion Router. Retrieved on May 28, 2011 from www.iusmentis.com/society/privacy/remailers/onionrouting/

Harris, R. (2006, July 11). Arriving at an Anti-Forensics Consensus: Examining How to Define and Control the Anti-Forensics Problem. Retrieved on May 28, 2011 from http://www.sciencedirect.com/science/article/pii/S1742287606000673

Harris, S., Harper, A., Eagle, C., and Ness, J. (2008). *Gray Hat Hacking: The Ethical Hacker's Handbook*, 2nd ed., pp. 203–204, McGraw-Hill Professional, New York, NY.

Hollister, S. (2011, February 2). Android 3.0 'Honeycomb' Can Encrypt All Your Data, Needs a Full Hour's Charge. In *Engaged*. Retrieved on May 28, 2011 from http://www.engadget.com/2011/02/02/android-3-0-honeycomb-can-encrypt-all-your-data-needs-a-full/

Johnson, N. F. (2011). Steganography Software. Retrieved on May 28, 2011 from http://www.jjtc.com/Steganography/tools.html

Mah, P. (2007, July 28). IronKey Flash Drive "Self-Destructs" on Too Many Failed Password Attempts. In *TechRepublic*. Retrieved on May 28, 2011 from http://www.techrepublic.com/blog/tech-news/ironkey-flash-drive-self-destructs-on-too-many-failed-password-attempts/916

McGill, L. (2005, May 5). Steganography: The Right Way. In *SANS*. Retrieved on May 28, 2011 from http://www.sans.org/reading_room/whitepapers/stenganography/steganography_1584

Milliron, B. (2010, October 15). Rootkit Investigation Procedures. In *SANS*. Retrieved on May 15, 2011 from http://www.sans.org/score/checklists/rootkits_investigation_procedures.pdf

Pajek, P., and Pimenidis, E. (2009, September 2). Computer Anti-Forensics Methods and Their Impact on Computer Forensic Investigation. Retrieved on May 28, 2011 from http://www.springerlink.com/content/t828395580666546/

Peron, C. S., and Legary, M. (2005). *Digital Anti-Forensics: Emerging Trends in Data Transformation Techniques*. Retrieved on May 28, 2011 from www.ide.bth.se/~andersc/kurser/DVC013/PDFs/Seccuris-Antiforensics.pdf

Ripe, and Pluf. (2005, January 8). Advanced Antiforensics: SELF. *Phrack*, 63(0x3f). Retrieved on May 28, 2011 from http://www.phrack.org/issues.html?issue=63&id=11#article

Rogers, M. K. (2005, September 15). Anti-Forensics. Retrieved on May 28, 2011 from http://www.cyberforensics.purdue.edu/documents/AntiForensics_LockheedMartin09152005.pdf#documents/AntiForensics_LockheedMartin09152005.pdf

Zadjmool, R. (2004, July 23). Hidden Threat: Alternate Data Streams. In *Windows Security*. Retrieved on May 28, 2011 from http://www.windowsecurity.com/articles/alternate_data_streams.html

12

Link and Visual Analysis

Introduction

The digital forensic process involves discovering information in an attempt to provide insight into actions and events. The details that explain what has occurred are often lacking, and in some situations almost nothing is known about what has happened. Sifting through digital media in an organized and methodical way can shed light on what has occurred, but there can be so many apparently unconnected pieces of information that developing a clear picture is nearly impossible. The usage of link and visual analysis (LAVA) techniques provides a way to organize and analyze the information pertinent to an investigation and develop a better understanding of the actions and events of interest.

Previously, we have reviewed a number of forensic tools and report writing. Currently, it has been shown that the computer forensic tools have expanded their focus from finding information to analyzing information. This means that the strength of forensic tools has been searching through volumes to recover files and artifacts. However, generally speaking, a weakness in forensic tools is that they have not been good at aggregating the information and presenting it in a way that aids in interpretation. Tools and techniques used in business intelligence and statistical analysis were not considered as part of the digital forensics world. The only commonly aggregated and shared information is hash sets.

Link and Visual Analysis

Files have several date and time (temporal) attributes including created time, modified time, and accessed time. This can allow for the temporal analysis of files by those attributes, which helps answer the question of who did what and when. What has not been easy to determine is "who did what and when" in situations when there are multiple computers, users, devices, and situations, nor has there been a way to look at trends and relationships. One of the reasons for this is that each device has its own image, and unless the images are accessible by the forensic tool it is impossible to use the tool to aggregate the information efficiently. For example, if the mobile devices were analyzed by Cellebrite and computers by using EnCase then bringing the information together is difficult. There are ways to get Cellebrite extract information into EnCase, but clearly EnCase is not a reporting and an analyzing tool similar to what is used in Business Intelligence. Accessed data utilize a database with FTK, which help in reporting, but there are still gaps in analysis capability.

LAVA tools take information and develop intelligence by finding links and correlations within the data. An example that helps put a face on LAVA is to walk through a cell phone scenario using i2. We have a situation where we need to analyze the calling patterns of four individuals. Figure 12.1 shows a chart representing the calls made in a month from the four individual's phones. Each icon represents a distinct phone number, and each line represents one or more phone calls. The direction of the arrow represents who made the call (where the call has been originated). An arrow toward a phone indicates a received call and an arrow away from a phone represents an initiated call.

The phone network diagram provides some sense as to the volume and direction of the calls, but the data could be cleared up. Simply by changing the way, the data are represented into an organizational diagram. Figure 12.2 illustrates the relationships among the four individuals of interest.

A potential pattern emerges within the organizational diagram where there is a clear path linking the four individuals together. We realize that there may be more people in this network who may clear things up even more, but at this point we have only four individuals. This is where a temporal analysis provides further insight. Temporal analysis is where the data are laid out on a timeline. We remember that in the previous examples that a single line between two phones indicated one or more calls between the individuals. A temporal analysis breaks this down further so that we can see when each of the calls was made. Figure 12.3 is a representation of the data from the previous examples transformed into a temporal view.

This represents the same information as shown in Figures 12.1 and 12.2, but filtered down to just the phone calls among the four phones of interest. In addition, a

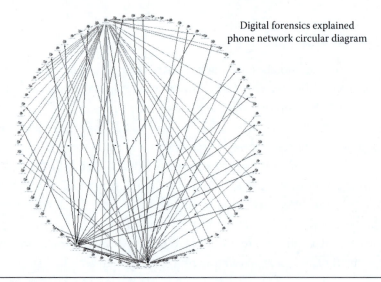

Digital forensics explained
phone network circular diagram

Figure 12.1   Phone network circular diagram.

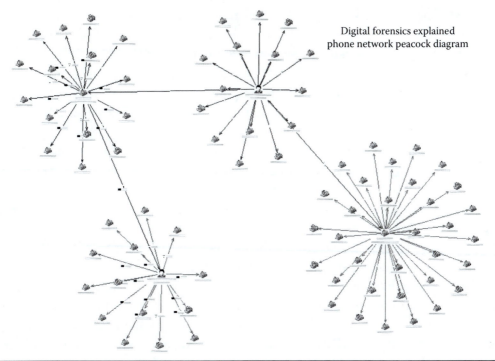

Digital forensics explained
phone network peacock diagram

Figure 12.2 Phone network organizational diagram.

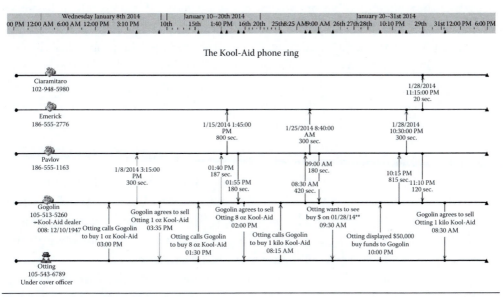

Figure 12.3 Phone network temporal view.

fifth phone, that of undercover detective Otting, has been included. The situation is that Det. Otting calls Gogolin at 3:00 PM on January 8 to buy 1 ounce of Kool-Aid. At 3:15 PM, Gogolin calls Pavlov to make sure that they have enough Kool-Aid, and then returns a call to Det. Otting to complete the sale arrangements. At 1:30 PM on January 15, Det. Otting calls Gogolin to see if he can buy 8 ounces of Kool-Aid. At

1:40 PM, Gogolin calls Pavlov to see if they have 8 ounces of Kool-Aid to sell. Pavlov calls Emerick at 1:45 PM because he needs more inventories to be able to make the sale. At 1:55 PM, Pavlov calls Gogolin back to indicate that they have enough inventories. At 2:00 PM, Gogolin calls Det. Otting to complete the sale arrangements. This scenario has been repeated twice more on January 25 and 28, thereby indicating a clear communication channel and strongly supports the probability that a Kool-Aid ring exists.

Figure 12.3 is a good example of LAVA, in which the lines representing the calls are links, and the way it has been laid out on a timeline enables the visual analysis. Other evidence can be layered into this chart including geographic information system (GIS) data, bank account information, and other activities and events that may be related. Although some forensic tools may get you partially to this type of picture, it is the ability to layer in or aggregate the information from multiple sources into one central location, which distinguishes the power of LAVA.

Further capabilities of LAVA include statistical analysis to provide predictive intelligence and perform other functions to assist the investigator with sorting through the pile of information that is frequently a part of digital forensic investigations. For example, tools such as THREADS can analyze calling or communication patterns to help determine the leader of a ring or gang. Factors such as length of call, who initiated the call, frequency of the calls, and time of the call related to other calls are used to analyze the hierarchy of an organization. For example, if Marco calls Julia for 45 seconds and then Marco calls Buddy 1 minute after completing the call with Julia—and this pattern is repeated three times during the month—the probability that the calls are related is very high. In addition, the probability that there is some sort of relationship between Julia and Marco is very high. On the contrary, if Marco calls Julia for 45 seconds and then 2 days later Marco calls Buddy, the probability that the two calls are related is small, and the likelihood that Julia and Buddy have some sort of relationship is also much smaller.

Social networks from digital sources such as Facebook, Twitter, and LinkedIn leave traces of activity on computers and mobile devices. These fragments may be beneficial in determining some social network identities and activities, but LAVA tools can help identify and analyze social network relationships. Because of the prevalence of digital social networking, obtaining a grasp on the members and relationships within the network is an important aspect of digital forensic investigation.

Some of the analysis factors in social networking include the four measures of Centrality: Betweenness, Closeness, Degree, and Eigenvector. All four measures of Centrality have a mathematical basis. Centrality looks at the location of something between two other points or objects. This can be used to help determine the relative importance or influence that someone possesses in a social network. Betweenness deals with a node's importance in a network—how central it is and how many relationships pass through it to get into another relationship. A node in a social network is a centering point such as a person or entity. A strong measure of Betweenness could be interpreted as someone being the center of a ring or a gang—very influential in the social network. A strong Betweenness score can also indicate that someone is a Gatekeeper, or they control communication in a network.

Closeness is the opposite of Farness. It is a measure of the proximity of relationships—how close they are in a network. Nodes with strong closeness scores are those that can communicate with other nodes the fastest because of their proximity. Degree Centrality is the number of links to a node. This could be indicative of how popular someone is in a network, but it is not necessarily a measure of how important someone is in a network. In a social setting, someone who has lot of connections has a high Degree of Centrality, which may be viewed as very popular. Similarly, someone who has few connections has a low Degree of Centrality—which may be viewed as unpopular. However, in an organizational setting, the leader may only have a few direct reports—so that they will have a much lower Degree of Centrality. Regardless, a higher Degree of Centrality score means that someone is active in a network.

Eigenvector Centrality measures the amount of influence that a node has in a network. The measure can be indicative of internal network influence and also influence leaving the network. So, the Eigenvector value informs how one might interpret the Degree of Centrality by taking into account how influential someone is.

The network in Figure 12.4 can be analyzed for Betweenness, Degree of Centrality, Closeness, and Eigenvector measures. Some LAVA packages calculate Betweenness, Degree of Centrality, Closeness, Eigenvector, and other measures, as do some statistical packages. This can be very useful when interpreting large networks. Figure 12.5 shows the Betweenness, Closeness, Degree, and Eigenvector values for each of the nodes in the network. The nodes having strong Betweenness are Sara JONES, Juan RODRIGUEZ, Frank EVERS, Betty BILFORD, and Tim JOHNSON, with Tim JOHNSON being the strongest score.

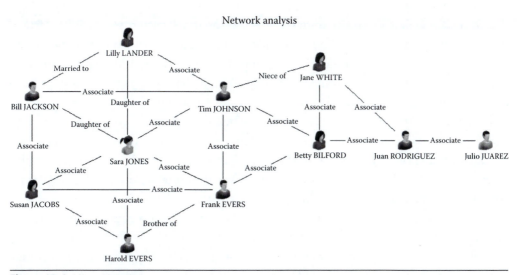

Figure 12.4 Network analysis.

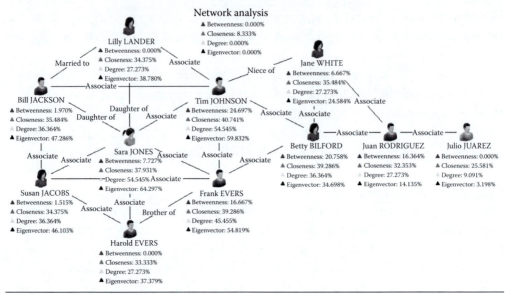

Figure 12.5   Network statistical analysis.

When you initially look at the network, the first inclination might be that Sara JONES is the center of the network, but the Betweenness score indicates that Tim JOHNSON is the most important node, followed by Betty BILFORD, Frank EVERS, and Juan RODRIGUEZ. Tim JOHNSON also has the highest Closeness score, which means that he is the closest in proximity when compared with all of the other nodes. Sara JONES and Tim JOHNSON have the highest Degree of Centrality score, which means that they are the most popular based on the network. Sara JONES has the highest Eigenvector score, followed by Tim JOHNSON. Remember, the Eigenvector measures the amount of influence on a network. Taking all of these measures together, Tim JOHNSON would certainly be a node of interest.

In addition to network analysis, this type of statistical analysis can be used to help determine the characteristics in digital crime such as attack patterns—including attack patterns in hacking incidents. These patterns provide insight that may tie crimes to the same perpetrator, as well as illuminate group dynamics. Statistical analysis provides quantitative data that cannot only confirm hypothesis that are a part of a digital forensics examination, but an analysis can also indicate that a hypothesis is not particularly well supported. You may recall in Chapter 1 when the scientific process was reviewed that I emphasized the importance of verifying results before reporting. Improperly reported findings can ruin the innocent people's lives and potentially enable the guilty to go unpunished. I cannot stress it enough—verify results before publishing, and a strong way to verify is by confirming the results with an alternative method.

LAVA has application in many fields including law enforcement, intelligence, finance, insurance, health care, and a variety of other areas where studying linkages and relationships helps provide situational insight. To reach full potential, the information in a LAVA environment should be coupled with a scalable database environment such as Oracle or Microsoft SQL Server. This would allow sharing of information among incidents, cases, examiners, analysts, and organizations. The insurance industry has been an early adopter of LAVA technology in rooting out insurance fraud. Someone that commits insurance fraud often switches insurance company targets, which makes it harder to find a fraudulent pattern. Insurance companies have done a far better job sharing information with other companies relative to insurance fraud. Other industries, including law enforcement, would do well to model after this cooperative information sharing approach. Many LAVA tools have interfaces to relational databases and information sharing services, but a concerted effort includes standardization needs to occur in order to achieve widespread success.

Artifacts and information from digital forensic investigations can also be shared among investigators and organizations through the usage of a database. Once in a database, this information can be mined for similarities and trends using LAVA tools viewing information from multiple cases and sources (a "Big Data" approach) rather than trying to find patterns by looking at single cases by themselves.

Conclusion

Continuing to work on digital forensic cases on a case-by-case approach is like trying to bail the *Titanic* with a bucket. A new approach is required to make headway and get ahead of the challenges in digital forensics. Sharing case information and evaluating it using LAVA tools shows promise in helping the investigators to work more effectively. Statistical techniques can be used to help validate the findings, direct investigators to the areas they may have overlooked, and provide focus via predictive analysis. LAVA is not a silver bullet, but it is an area that can significantly improve the efficiency and effectiveness of digital forensic investigators.

13

PSYCHOLOGICAL, ETHICAL, AND CULTURAL IMPLICATIONS OF DIGITAL FORENSICS

Introduction

Of all the books that I have read dealing with digital forensics, coverage of psychology, ethics, and culture seems to be completely overlooked. As I work on the cases, it becomes clear to me that these areas are the central aspects of digital forensic investigations. What I want to cover in this chapter would be not only the psychological aspects of the person(s) being investigated but also the psychological aspects of the investigator. An investigator faces many ethical questions, many of which present themselves later on in the examination. Finally, many cultural issues include fairly basic things such as language and idiomatic expressions, and they also include the understanding of the cultural conceptual framework that encompasses an incident. When I have discussions with the investigators about language and cultural issues, they often dismiss the challenge as something that can be handled with a language translation tool. But to me, this is an oversimplification and complete misunderstanding of a complex situation.

Psychological Implications of Digital Forensics

Undoubtedly, the area in digital forensics where I felt the most underprepared was the psychological factors. As I did undergraduate and graduate degrees in computer information systems and had about 20 years of experience in IT when I entered the forensics area, I found the technical challenges in adapting to forensics to be fairly easy. Obtaining a stronger understanding of various file systems was perhaps the only significant technical learning curve. Certainly, there were some process and methodological things to work out, but in terms of effort, the technical jumping was not much different than the jumping from mainframe to client/server or from client/server to web. I had taken psychology and sociology classes when obtaining a biology degree, and at one time I had majored in criminal justice, so I took classes on deviant behavior and domestic situations. But even that did not prepare me for what presents itself in digital forensics. There are some really twisted people and situations out there and it really takes a toll.

One of the ways that I thought would help provide some sense of what I mean by psychological implications of digital forensics would be to simply walk through some of the situations and scenarios that I have encountered as a way to provide some semblance of approximate situations that a digital forensic investigator may encounter. A friend of mine who attended the Air Force Academy explained that part of pilot training involves psychological exercises. Pilots have to answer the questions in their mind before they go on sorties so that when they reach the action point they are able to respond appropriately. They cannot just fly a bomber to a location and then decide whether or not they can drop the bombs. Those questions have to be answered before getting into the cockpit. Similarly, there are things that a digital forensic investigator has to decide up front. Each investigator has to determine what types of cases they will be able to work as well as how to work on them.

When someone decides to pursue digital forensics, it is often the appeal of sexy technology that attracts them—not necessarily any particular type of case. The type of cases that someone works largely depends on their career path. Local law enforcement spends considerable time dealing with child porn (CP). Corporate investigators may deal with the human resources department doing things like reviewing the computer of employees who have recently left the employer. They may also deal with the incident response of a computer breach. Private investigators often deal with the civil and domestic cases, with much of the work focused on divorce situations. It is not to say that each of the previously described environments may be different than I described, but the investigator should be aware of what they are getting themselves into.

Literally speaking, the way I like to describe the digital forensics is that it is a look into someone's soul. As you go through and recover deleted files, pictures, e-mail, internet history and timelines, a pretty clear picture of an individual begins to emerge. The habits, preferences, and affinities crystallize as the patterns emerge. Within a short period of time, it is not uncommon to develop a sense as to whether this is the type of person you could get along with, or if this is the type of person that you begin to loathe. That alone can subconsciously influence an investigation. Another aspect that often emerges fairly quickly is whether or not you have been presented with details that coincide with what is on the device being investigated. The adage that "there are two sides to every story" certainly applies, and if the device being investigated is shared by many people, there are likely many sides to the story and it may be very difficult to make sense of things.

The cases that I am going to describe will be veiled so that confidentiality is not breached. They may be either a combination of many cases, academic cases, or they may be fictional representations. However, they do represent common situations. The reason I want to include cases is that it is important for people understand the environment. Once I had a high-school student who asked to job shadow me when I was a computer programmer in the mid-1980s. I asked her what she wanted me to show her and she indicated that she just wanted to watch me work like I normally would if she was not there. Programming can be quite a contemplation process at times, and when she came into job shadow, it was one of those times. I was working on an insurance underwriting system and was developing some mathematical models. After watching me for 15 minutes as I alternated between typing and thinking (which I often did while looking at the ceiling), she abruptly got up from her chair and said that programming looked boring, she did not want to be a programmer, and left. I guess it was good that she figured out that she did not want to be a programmer before she spent much time on it, but she also did not really get an accurate idea of what a career as a programmer was.

As anyone in the computer field knows, there are frequent calls from friends and others asking for what amounts to free help. Almost never does the request results in something that can be addressed quickly. From a forensic standpoint, this is compounded. One of the most common requests is to recover files that were deleted accidently. Usually, the files are pictures. A technique that is often used to recover deleted pictures is to carve the files using a global regular expression print (GREP) search on graphic file headers. This will recover all of the graphic files available for recovery, which may be more than what the person wanted to be recovered and can result in an embarrassing situation because graphic files from the Internet are also recovered.

The technical developments in digital forensics occur at a rapid rate. As such, frequent ongoing education is necessary. Training situations can provide an opportunity for the investigators to network and commiserate on things they have run into. I know one investigator who mentioned that a neighbor asked him to put in a new hard drive, as the original had crashed. After changing out the hard drive and getting the computer up and running, the investigator asked the neighbor what he wanted to be done with the old drive. The neighbor told him that he did not care, so the investigator took it home and placed it on a shelf in his garage. About a year later, he was in need of a hard drive and remembered the drive in the garage. He retrieved it and hooked it up to the forensic tools to check whether it was usable or not. What he found was a hard drive full of CP. His neighbor was serving 10 years in the state penitentiary. Now this might seem to be the end of the story, but think about the neighborhood these two people lived in. The environment is changed forever including friendships and the way the people are treated. The child victims should be remembered as well. There is no ideal outcome in a case like this.

There are a lot of people with eBay and craigslist stories. It is amazing what you can find on these types of sights, and even more amazing is that the people would even consider selling things such as old computers. I will always tell people to at least remove the hard drive if they are about to sell a computer. One of my friends is a craigslist junkie. He is constantly buying, selling, and trading things on craigslist. On one occasion, he bought a used computer of craigslist, and as he had only modest computer skills, he asked me if I would take a quick look at it to make sure there was nothing on it that should not be. We hooked the computer up to some forensic tools and found that it was full of homemade satanic porn, complete with blood involvement.

These types of disturbing images will be ingrained in your mind just as deeply as any kind of case you encounter.

Private sector digital forensic investigators should make contact with law enforcement and develop relationships because sooner or later the two paths will cross. Sooner or later non-law enforcement digital forensic investigators will encounter situations that will need to be turned over to law enforcement. In somewhat rural settings, or even at the state level, law enforcement may need assistance with digital forensic cases from those outside of law enforcement. The reality is that most law enforcement agencies have limited training and expertise (Gogolin and Jones, 2010). The environment that you encounter in a law enforcement situation may be the one where a suspect is in the custody and you need to quickly examine the digital media for related evidence. I have been in situations where I am quickly working through various devices and I can hear people yelling and raising a commotion from the holding area. This by itself can be quite unnerving. The reason behind the request for assistance can be unsettling because in law enforcement situations, digital forensic investigators are often dealing with sex offenders. As conditions of parole, sex offenders are often required not to frequent particular types of websites or to have pictures of certain individuals. Even if the conditions of parole are met, it is still quite common to find the images that you would rather not see. After a while, for some examiners dealing with these types of cases can become somewhat routine and it can be almost like performing any other investigative task. However for others, the psychological toll can be too high to justify and a career redirection is necessary.

Law enforcement may rely on digital evidence for assistance with an unsolved crime. An example case that comes to mind is a middle-school girl who had a picture in her iPod of the person who reportedly abducted her. The girl knew the abductor and actually recruited him for an intimate encounter through social media. The iPod was recovered in a locked state, and nobody had any idea where the girl might be. Different types of devices have different types of security controls, some are easy to circumvent whereas the others are boarder line impossible. The time to learn how to do this is not in a pressure situation such as in the middle of a child abduction. Contacts with hardware vendors should be established so that the process is understood, precious time is not wasted, and skills should be practiced proactively. The outcome of cases such as this can be particularly troubling, and if the investigator handles things inefficiently and the outcome is unfavorable, there can be ongoing psychological impacts on the investigator. By the same token, if the investigator is prepared the chance for a favorable outcome is more likely, which can turn into far better psychological impact.

The previously described cases are generally quick hitters. You are in and out in minutes-to-hours. The types of cases that can be most perplexing are often those whose duration runs in weeks or months. The cases can take many twists and turns, and the ongoing day-to-day drudgery of dealing with the situation in an ongoing manner can be psychologically draining. An example of a case that fits this description brings to mind a particular divorce case. The husband and wife were the co-owners of a hardware store in a mountain community, when the wife became suspicious of the husband's erratic behavior. Examination of the family computer revealed e-mail and other evidence of the husband's affairs. During the course of the e-mail investigation, it became evident that the husband was also into exchanging media from a large porn collection. On further examination, it became evident that the husband was interested in young girls, with many pictures of girls who were young in appearance and in inappropriate situations. The most troubling was the discovery of a large number of pictures of anime CP, with many images of children who were appearing to be preschool or younger.

One of the issues at stake in this case was that of child custody, and the couple had several young children including an adolescent female. The child was unaware of the specifics of the forensic investigation, but the husband was playing on the emotions of the girl to make it appear that he was the victim and her mother was really the one with ill intent. The prosecutor in the jurisdiction who normally handles this type of case was on extended leave that just happened to almost exactly coincide with the approximately 6-month duration of the investigation. Many jurisdictions do not prosecute anime or animated CP cases as the interpretation is that there is no victim. However, some jurisdictions do not interpret anime and animated images as victimless and do pursue. The prosecutor who would make the determination in this case was not available, and the criminal charges were not pursued at that time. However, the case expanded to include business computers and other digital devices, and it became clear to the civil court that the husband did have psychological problems and custody rights were correspondingly terminated. Clearly, there were difficult mental challenges for a number of people in this case. The psychological toll on the investigator in dealing a case like this, where the outcome was not a complete failure but was less than favorable, which resulted in sleepless nights for an extended period of time.

Frustration is something that can manifest itself in many ways. There can be cases where the investigation clearly reveals laws being broken, but the legal system declines to take the case. This may be due to any number of factors including current work load, experience with similar cases, lack of understanding of the technology involved, or even political motivations. One of the most frustrating cases that comes to mind was an embezzlement case, where someone stole millions of dollars from an elderly individual under the pretense of help in asset management of the elderly person. The embezzler converted the assets to cash and then went to great lengths to hide the money trail. At about the time when the elderly person became aware that virtually all assets were gone, the embezzler died suddenly. The pattern of activity illustrated a high probability that several people were accomplices, but on the surface there was nothing concrete. I was brought in by the elderly person's legal team to help uncover the embezzlement network and perhaps jump start a criminal case. Relatives of the embezzler were selling assets that may have been acquired from the embezzlement activity. There were considerable auction house, eBay, and craigslist activity, and things were being sold at well below the market value.

The first thing that I was interested in was the embezzler's computer. Just as I was beginning my investigation, it appeared that the embezzler was also a child pornographer and the computer had to be turned over to law enforcement. As the suspect was dead, the procedure was to destroy all digital media that may contain CP. This effectively destroyed all the evidence and no charges were ever pursued against any of the suspects. People had been from being penniless to walking away multimillionaires. The thing that made this case and the civil/child custody case as previously described particularly disturbing is that embezzler and the husband in the previous case were both conspicuous Christians. The embezzler appeared to be using the stolen proceeds to purchase tens of thousands of dollars worth of religious artifacts. The husband leveraged his position within his church to develop relationships with vulnerable women and then pursue them sexually. As a Christian, I found this behavior not only despicable, but it also cast a very negative shadow on Christianity itself. So, investigators should be prepared for situations where the subject of their pursuit desecrates things they value. Investigators commonly call these people "bad guys," but you may come up with your own vernacular.

There are many times when the investigator working a case is not surprised to find CP or other disturbing material. In those situations, the investigator is able to prepare his/her mind in advance and it may not be a shock when the details are discovered. However, in a case where it is not expected and troubling details are discovered, the best way that I can describe the situation is like falling through the ice on an ice-covered lake. It can happen in slow motion and then you find yourself shocked and underwater, trying to swim toward the light. Suddenly feeling cold—very cold—is not an uncommon reaction. This may soon be replaced by an urge to help the children, although there may be almost no way to effectively do this, particularly in an international situation. The satisfaction from these types of cases comes from the reality that CP cases that are investigated correctly often have a strong prosecution outcome, and that the person in possession of the material, even if not the creator, meets a stiff sentence.

Another investigative aspect that should be noted is that in some cases, the investigator may be acquainted with the person you are investigating. This can be more common in a corporate setting where cases can have an internal focus. When this situation occurs, an investigator has to decide if it is possible to proceed objectively or if the investigation should be turned over to someone else.

An investigator needs to have coping skills to help them deal with the mental hurdles that an investigation can encounter. Often times the investigator cannot talk about the case, so they have to keep the case specifics bottled up for extended periods of time. Coping mechanisms include counseling, exercise routines, journaling, and other techniques. This can allow an investigator to spend at least some of the emotional energy that a case can involve and help to reduce stress. It is important that an investigator has to be proactive in case stress levels and emotional strain grows unchecked. Family members may not understand this and it may compound the situation. Being aware of the potential issues is the first step toward effectively managing them.

There are many more psychological considerations that could be covered, many with ethical overtones, but one more area to touch on involves findings. An investigator has to be absolutely sure of the results and not to read more or less into what is found than the evidence supports. If a computer is used by many people then it can be very difficult to tie a particular activity to one person with 100% certainty. The way investigation results are interpreted can forever change the lives of many people and that point should never be forgotten. Similarly, investigators have to decide what types of cases they are willing to work and understand the implications of taking certain cases.

Ethical Implications of Digital Forensics

Each investigator has to determine what will be their personal code of ethics. Once a line is crossed, it is impossible to go back. We have covered some of the psychological aspects dealing with stress and emotion, but there are several similar ethical aspects. There has been much written regarding ethics, and the purpose is not to revisit or repackage that vast body of work. The objective of this section is to point out some things having ethical connotations that might not be at the forefront of current discussion about ethics but still need to be considered.

The first thing that I discuss with people who are interested in digital forensics is that there is an incredible power not only with the tools, but also with the information that can be captured. With this power comes great responsibility because the investigator has the ability to shape how the information is presented and perceived; and in many cases, people accept the findings as concrete. Investigators have to stick to the facts and not attempt to color the interpretations or influence the situation by not presenting the full picture. For example, it is easy to say that a particular file was found on someone's computer. But that is not presenting the full picture if there is a possibility that the computer was used by more than one person or that it is possible the file was the result of malware and not an action by the computer's owner.

Another aspect that deals with ethics but is also a good investigative practice is simply verifying results. Presenting findings before verification can lead to a situation similar to trying to put the genie back into the bottle. The more serious the findings and implications, the more strenuously they should be verified. Verification by a second party and/or multiple confirming processes are the possible methods. Context of the findings and the computers in use are other considerations that can influence verification.

Good ethical practices and good investigative practices are complimentary, even when looking at things from an analytical perspective. People often ask what traits are common in a good investigator. My response is an ethical person who likes to work on puzzles, can apply the scientific method, and can objectively come up with competitive theories to explain situations. The definition of forensics is the application of science to answer a question, and it often deals with a large number of unknown facts. By applying scientific principles, the investigator seeks to reveal the facts. Competitive theory involves coming up with multiple explanations for an occurrence or phenomenon, not getting tunnel vision and going down the path of the most convenient explanation. The goal of competitive theory is not to put all the eggs in one basket and rush to judgment, but rather to look at multiple perspectives. This is particularly important in a case that may go to trial because competitive theories can be presented by the opposing side, and if the investigator has already considered the theories presented then that will be much easier to be addressed. Similarly, an investigation can be a life altering experience for the person who is under investigation. If wrongly accused, irreparable damage may have been done. Performing shoddy work and/or wrongly accusing someone can be among the most unethical situations examiners can place themselves in. Presenting information that later turns out to be inaccurate or incorrect can ruin many lives and families.

A topic that I stress in every forensic class is that you should never investigate your family. I cannot tell you how many people have told me that they have tried out various forensic tools and supporting technologies on their family members or people they know. Not only is this unethical, in many cases it is also illegal. Use of keyloggers, phone tracking/tapping software, and similar tools in many cases is a felony and perhaps a federal crime. As I have already mentioned, when you use a forensic tool you look into someone's soul. Many times there is no context to frame what you find, which can create misinterpretation. You may not like what you find and, as Bob Seger sings in "Against the Wind," "I wish I didn't know now what I didn't know then."

One last ethical aspect that I have not seen a lot in the literature but I have seen in practice is making personal copies of things found on other's machines. This may be something simple like an mp3, picture, or video file, or something more extensive such as licensed software. Just because an examiner has access to something does not mean they are free to make copies. Forensic examiners are like bank tellers—they get to touch the money but they do not get to keep it. Always remember that ethics includes trust and integrity. If either of them is lost then they may never be recaptured.

Cultural Implications of Digital Forensics

It would be interesting to try and measure the impact of the internet on culture. Relatively, few people used the World Wide Web before the late 1990s, but now it is ubiquitous. Social media, virtual worlds, online gaming, and e-mail are just a few of the technologies that have brought the world to our fingertips. Because of the ease at which we can be drawn together, cultural understanding is much more important. We need to understand that idiomatic expressions, slang, and gestures can have far different interpretation than originally intended. It also means that crimes can be committed by someone on the other side of the world. Gone are the days of bank robbers being confined to local or regional areas. Gone are the days of bullies being limited to just the distance of earshot. We are in a different world and failing to adapt to the changing conditions has serious repercussions. A terrorist could have the instructions on how to hijack an airliner on his smartphone. Even if a transportation security administration (TSA) agent inspects the phone when would be hijacker boards the plane, if the instructions are simply written in plain text in a foreign language then the agent is likely to overlook the evidence. The same could be said about the instructions being in an e-mail message on a laptop.

Digital forensic is one of the key technologies of cyber security. It can be used for testing, verification, incident response, and analysis. Because of the global nature of the digital world, it is not possible for one person or even one country to fully grasp the challenges that are present. Digital forensics and cyber crime are multidisciplinary areas that require expertise in several areas including law, computer science, finance networking, data mining, and criminal justice (Goel, 2010). In addition to that, most countries have multiple dialects and languages that are commonly spoken. Relatively few people in the United States are fluent in more than one language. In an Associated Press article (2005), it was reported that half of Europeans were bilingual whereas only 9% of Americans were familiar with more than one language. In 2010, Francois Grosjean found it difficult to quantify bilingualism, but estimated that 56% of Europe, 38% of Great Britain, 35% of Canada, and 17% of the United States are qualified as bilingual. The implications of language and culture on cyber security cannot be understated. In a 2010 article, Coopes indicated that the global cyber crime problem is larger than the global drug trade. In Australia, it has been reported that an identity is stolen every 3 seconds (Coopes, 2010). A cyber crime investigation involves a potentially large number of individuals and groups, who need to communicate, share, and make decisions across many levels and boundaries (Katos and Bednar, 2008). Not to think there are multicultural issues at play is to put one's head in the sand. As one of the key ways to investigate cyber crime incidents is through digital forensics, cultural understanding, and language skills may be what distinguishes a good investigator from a great investigator.

Family situations are often largely constructed around culture. In many areas of the world, multiple generations live in the same house. In many cultures such as those with Spanish heritage, families and friends get together far more than the typical American family. So, the reason to explain why certain individuals are together can have a cultural basis. It is these kinds of insights that an investigator has to understand when examining digital devices. There can be many explanations for events, communications, and digital images that are located on the media. There can be many mothers in one household, and without this understanding the meaning of messages can be misconstrued.

Another aspect to surface when discussing culture is that it can provide an appreciation of what someone is thinking and how they might act or what techniques they might use to obfuscate evidence. Gaining this understanding can help to establish motive and method that are the keys to any digital forensic investigation. Being able to converse in a foreign language with a suspect opens many investigative doors. Without taking the time to study and understand culture, many of these clues and opportunities would be overlooked. Examiners need every edge they can get because forensic investigations are difficult enough just by their very nature.

Conclusion

This chapter covered a lot of deep subjects, and I will be the first to admit that I do not have a degree in psychology and little formal training in ethics. However, the degree to which they impact the digital forensic process and the investigators conducting the examinations are often overlooked. Few technical books devote time to psychology, ethics, and culture—at least culture in the popular sense. Subcultures in various technologies and movements do receive mention on occasion. But to learn culture and be able to converse in multiple languages takes time and discipline, and unfortunately very few technical curricula require fluency in foreign language. This oversight has the potential to hamstring the ability to plan for and react to digital incidents such as breaches in cyber security and technologically aided crimes. Just like communication skills are key business competencies, language and cultural skills are key cyber security and digital forensic investigative competencies.

References

Associated Press. (2005). Half of Europe's Citizens Know 2 Languages. Retrieved on March 10, 2011 from http://www.breitbart.com/article.php?id=D8CQJUE02&show_article=1.

Coopes, A. (2010). Bigger than the Global Drug Trade, and Growing Quickly. Retrieved on February 14, 2011 from http://www.vancouversun.com/news/Bigger+than+global+drug+trade+growing+quickly/4028436/story.html#ixzz1F4jK2uyw.

Goel, S. (2010). Digital Forensics and Cyber Crime: First International ICST Conference, ICDF2C 2009, Albany, NY, USA, September 30–October 2, 2009, Revised Selected Papers. Lecture Notes of the Institute for Computer Sciences, Social Informatics and Telecommunications Engineering (1st ed.), Springer Publishing Company, Incorporated, Albany, NY.

Gogolin, G., and Jones, J. (January 2010). Law Enforcement's Ability to Deal with Digital Crime and the Implications for Business. *Information Security Journal: A Global Perspective* 19(3), 109–117.

Grosjean, F. (2010). *Bilingual: Life and Reality*. Harvard University Press, Boston, MA.

Katos, V., and Bednar, P. (May 2008). A Cyber-Crime Investigation Framework. *Computer Standards and Interfaces* 30(4), 223–228. http://0-dx.doi.org.libcat.ferris.edu/10.1016/j.csi.2007.10.003.

Index